THE CRIMINAL LAW
OF SCOTLAND

by

GERALD H. GORDON

Q.C., LL.D.

Sheriff of Glasgow and Strathkelvin, sometime
Professor of Scots Law in the University of Edinburgh

FIRST SUPPLEMENT
TO THE SECOND EDITION
Up to date to May 1, 1984

Published under the auspices of
THE SCOTTISH UNIVERSITIES' LAW INSTITUTE

EDINBURGH
W. GREEN & SON LTD.
1984

Published in 1984

ISBN Main work 0 414 00618 6
ISBN First supplement 0 414 00740 9

Typeset by John G. Eccles, Inverness
Printed in Great Britain by
Thomson Litho, East Kilbride

PREFACE

This supplement is intended to bring the law up to date as at May 1, 1984.

GERALD H. GORDON

Glasgow
May 1984

TABLE OF CASES

TABLE OF STATUTES

(References to repealed provisions are omitted except where the old law is discussed.
References in bold type indicate that all or most of the statutory text is quoted.)

PRIVATE ACTS

STATUTORY INSTRUMENTS

Note — The numbers in bold type in the left hand margin refer to paragraphs of the main work.

INTRODUCTION

0-09   Add new section:
A note on maximum penalties

0-10   Certain changes have been made in the maximum penalties available on summary conviction of statutory offences as a result of the Criminal Justice Act 1982 which inserts into the 1975 Act new sections 289B, 289F and 289G. These complicated provisions are discussed in Renton and Brown, 5th edition, paras. 1-05a, 17-03a and b, and 17-22a-d. Statements of penalties in the main work and this supplement must be read subject to these provisions, of which the most important are as follows.

0-11   (1) *Indictable offences*
(i) The maximum penalties available on 10th April 1983 on summary conviction of an indictable statutory offence created by an enactment passed not later than the session in which the Criminal Law Act 1977 was passed are to be amended according to the following table, unless provision is expressly made by any enactment for a larger penalty: s. 289B(1). For a discussion of the meaning, if any, of that exception, see Renton and Brown (5th edition), para. 17-03a.
(ii) Where different fines are provided on a first and on subsequent summary convictions, the largest fine is now available on any summary conviction: s. 298B(2).

Column 1	*Column 2*
Penalty or maximum penalty at commencement of section 55 of Criminal Justice Act 1982	*New maximum penalty*
1. Fine (other than a fine specified in paragraph 3 below, or a fine in respect of each period of a specified length during which a continuing offence is committed).	1. Fine not exceeding the prescribed sum.
2. Imprisonment for a period exceeding 3 months.	2. Imprisonment for a period not exceeding 3 months.

| 3. Fine in respect of a specified quantity or number of things. | 3. Fine not exceeding the prescribed sum in respect of each such quantity or number. |
| 4. Fine exceeding £100 in respect of each period of a specified length during which a continuing offence is committed. | 4. Fine not exceeding £100 in respect of each such period. |

The prescribed sum was originally £1,000, but was increased to £2,000 with effect from 1st May 1984, by the Increase of Criminal Penalties etc. (Scotland) Order 1984. The maximum fine available on summary conviction of any indictable offence mentioned in the principal work or in this supplement is therefore £2,000, unless a larger amount is stated.

0-12
(2) *Summary offences* (see Renton and Brown, para. 1-05a)
(i) Where any Act passed on or before 29th July 1977 (the date of the passing of the Criminal Law Act 1977) provides a maximum fine of less than £1,000 for a summary offence, and that fine has not been altered by the Criminal Law Act 1977, or by Schedule 7D to the 1975 Act, as inserted by Schedule 6 to the Criminal Justice Act 1982 with effect from 11th April 1983, or by any legislation between those dates, then, except for fines for each period of a specified length during which a continuing offence is committed, the fine was increased with effect from 11th April 1983 in accordance with the following table: s. 289F(8).

Column 1 Fine or maximum fine	Column 2 Increased amount
Under £25	£25
Under £50 but not less than £25	£50
Under £200 but not less than £50	£200
Under £400 but not less than £200	£500
Under £1,000 but not less than £400	£1,000

(ii) Almost all fines for summary offences are now expressed in terms of levels on a standard scale and not in monetary amounts. The original standard scale was as follows: s. 289G(2).

Standard Scale	
Level	Amount
1	£25
2	£50
3	£200
4	£500
5	£1,000

The amounts in the second column were doubled with effect from 1st May 1984: Increase of Criminal Penalties etc. (Scotland) Order 1984.

The result of all this is that where, for example, the maximum fine for a summary offence had not been increased by the Criminal Law Act 1977, or between the passing of that Act and 11th April 1983, and was £400 at that date, it was increased to £1,000 then by the table in s. 289F(8) of the 1975 Act. At the same time it was translated into a fine of level 5 in accordance with the table in s. 289G(2) of that Act. When the monetary equivalents of the levels were doubled on 1st May 1984,

0-12   it was increased to £2,000, while remaining a fine of level 5.

The scale does not apply to fines for each period of a specified length of time during which a continuing offence is committed, nor to the Companies Act 1981 or enactments mentioned in Sched. 2 to the Companies Act 1980: s. 289G(8).

0-13   (iii) Where different penalties are provided for a first and for subsequent convictions, the largest penalty is now available on any conviction: s. 289E.

0-14   References in this work to fines of a given level are references to fines for summary offences, the level being the level on the standard scale.

CHAPTER 1

CRIMES, OFFENCES AND THE DECLARATORY POWER

1-04   In *R* v. *Hull Visitors, ex p. Germain* [1979] 1Q.B. 425, 452A, Shaw, L.J. spoke of "the essential characteristic of a criminal cause or matter, namely, that it is a penal proceeding for the infraction of a requirement relating to the enforcement and preservation of public law and order."

Footnote 6. *McGregor* v. *T.* is now reported at 1975 S.C. 14.

Footnote 8. *Cordiner, Petr.* is now reported at 1973 J.C. 16.

1-06   Footnote 9. See now Renton and Brown, 5th ed., pp. 213-216.

Footnote 11. See now Renton and Brown, 5th ed., pp. 232-234.

1-13   In *Marcel Beller Ltd.* v. *Hayden* [1978] Q.B. 694, which concerned the interpretation of a clause in a life insurance policy which excluded death caused by "a criminal act", it was held that the offences of driving dangerously and driving while unfit through drink were "criminal acts", and would be included as such even if the exclusion were limited to crimes of moral culpability or turpitude.

1-26   It is now accepted that to have intercourse with a woman too drunk to give or refuse consent, where she has not been made drunk by the accused, is to commit indecent assault, and the same would apply to intercourse with a sleeping woman: *Sweeney and Anr.* v. *X.*, 1982 S.C.C.R. 509. See *infra*, para. 33-21.

1-32   Parliament has now declared that private sexual activity between consenting adult males is not criminal: Criminal Justice (Scotland) Act 1980, s. 80.

Shameless indecency was long thought of as a description of certain forms of behaviour between two or more persons, present together in one place, with at least one of them indulging in some kind of sexual behaviour directed towards the other or others. Lord Maxwell said in *Dean* v. *John Menzies (Holdings) Ltd.*, 1981 J.C. 23 at 38, that he supposed "that in the past the crime usually concerned actual physical conduct of the human body"; and, on the supposition that shameless indecency is *a* crime, it did concern itself with that. The crime has, however, recently been extended to cover quite different situations. This process began in *Watt* v. *Annan*, 1978 J.C. 84, where what the accused had done was to exhibit an obscene film to a number of adult males, *i.e.* run a stag movie night, and he was charged with conducting himself in a shamelessly indecent manner and exhibiting "a film of an obscene or indecent nature which was liable to create depraved, inordinate and lustful desires in those watching it and to corrupt the morals of the lieges." Macdonald's dictum was approved, and it was said that it was for Parliament and not the courts to set limits to it. The converse argument, that any application of the dictum (which technically could have no authority other than as a generalisation of common law decisions) to behaviour of a kind so different from that envisaged by Macdonald could be made only by Parliament, clearly did not find favour with the court. Lord Cameron said at page 89:

> "Whether or not conduct which is admittedly indecent or obscene is to be held criminal will depend on proof of the necessary *mens rea* and upon the facts and circumstances of the particular case. It would be impracticable as well as undesirable to attempt to define precisely the limits and ambit of this particular offence, far less to decide that the nature of the premises or place in which the conduct charged has occurred should alone be decisive in transforming conduct which would otherwise be proper subject of prosecution into conduct which may do no more than offend the canons of personal propriety or standards of contemporary morals. If it were considered desirable or necessary that this was a chapter of the criminal law in which precise boundaries or limits were to be set then the task is one which is more appropriate for the hand of the legislator."

The only limitation on the crime of shameless indecency is, as Lord Cameron put it, at pages 88-89, that:

> "It was accepted, and rightly so, in the submission for the Crown that the conduct to be criminal, in such circumstances as the facts in the present case disclose, must be directed towards some person or persons with an intention or knowledge that it should corrupt or be calculated or liable to corrupt or deprave those towards whom the indecent or obscene conduct was directed."

The offence was further extended in a series of cases (especially *Robertson* v. *Smith*, 1980 J.C. 1) so as to apply to circumstances virtually indistinguishable from those of the statutory offence of selling or exposing for sale obscene material, the purpose of the Crown in seeking such an extension being apparently to circumvent the smallness of the penalty then provided by Parliament for that statutory offence. The crime in such a case is described as selling, exposing for sale and having for sale, indecent and obscene books likely to deprave and corrupt the morals of the lieges and to create in their minds inordinate and lustful desires. The view of the court was that simply to expose for sale material known to be obscene, *i.e.* corrupting, constituted shameless indecency.

Despite its rapid and apparently successful development (on which see Gerald H. Gordon, "Shameless Indecency and Obscenity" (1980) 25 J.L.S. 262; G. Maher, "The Enforcement of Morals Continued", 1978 S.L.T. (News) 281; J.B. Stewart, "Obscenity Prosecutions", 1982 S.L.T. (News) 93; I.D. Willock, "Shameless Indecency — How Far has the Crown Office Reached?" (1981) 52 SCOLAG Bul. 199) it may be that this offence does not have much of a future. Its practical use is much limited by the decision in *Dean* v. *John Menzies (Holdings) Ltd.,*

1-32 *supra*, that it cannot be committed by a corporation, and the need to resort to it has been much reduced by the provision of substantial penalties for the statutory offence of dealing in obscene materials contrary to s. 51 of the Civic Government (Scotland) Act 1982. The *John Menzies* case also disturbed the theoretical basis of the whole development. Lord Cameron, who gave the opinions of the court in *Watt* v. *Annan, supra,* and *Robertson* v. *Smith, supra,* said in *John Menzies* that the shamelessness libelled in an obscenity case was objective, consisting of conduct known to be corrupting, and so was something with which the moral obliquity of the actor had nothing to do: 1981 J.C. at 32. The majority, however, while accepting *Robertson* v. *Smith,* held that all forms of shameless indecency did indeed require shamelessness and indecency in a subjective sense. The accused must, said Lord Stott, be "so lost to any sense of shame" as to authorise the sale of the material: at 36; and Lord Maxwell said that a finding of guilt implied that the accused had used his judgment and discretion in deciding to sell the material "in an indecent and shameless fashion": at 38. If these are requirements of shameless indecency it becomes very difficult to support *Robertson* v. *Smith,* and perhaps only a little less difficult to support *Watt* v. *Annan* — certainly they make the crime more difficult to prove than would the approach of Lord Cameron which requires no more than is needed to prove that the accused knowingly sold articles held by the court to be obscene.

The result of *John Menzies (Holdings) Ltd.* may be, therefore, to introduce some common sense into what was described by Lord Stott in that case as "an area of law in which (as is perhaps indicated by the archaic and faintly ludicrous wording of the complaint) commonsense is not noticeably at a premium": 1981 J.C. at 37. Lord Maxwell in that case expressed sympathy with the view that "in the realm of what is in substance censorship of certain types of magazines, literature, films etc. on the grounds that they are socially unacceptable, it would perhaps be preferable that the matter be dealt with by statute rather than the existing common law, which was I think designed to meet rather different problems": 1981 J.C. at 38. It may be that the strange eruption of shameless indecency into the already peculiar field of obscenity will come to be seen as merely a temporary crop which withered and died under the attack of *Dean* v. *John Menzies (Holdings) Ltd.*

In *Sommerville* v. *Tudhope,* 1981 J.C. 58 the High Court declined to hold that it was a crime for a wholesaler to possess obscene material for distribution to retailers, on the ground that the public did not resort to wholesale premises so that no affront to public decency or morals was involved. It was said that the penalisation of the mere possession of pornography, as distinct from its exposure for sale, involved "issues of public and social policy which . . . are for the legislature to resolve, but not to be resolved by an unwarranted extension of the common law.": at 64.

1-34 *Dalton* was followed in *Dean* v. *Stewart,* 1980 S.L.T. (Notes) 85 where it was held to be an attempt to pervert the course of justice to give the police false information as to the identity of the driver of a car which had failed to stop after an accident.

1-39   *Kerr* v. *Hill* was approved by the Court of Appeal in *R.* v. *Thomas (Derek)* [1979] Q.B. 326 where it was held to be an attempt to pervert the course of justice to make a false accusation. Wasting the time of the police by falsely reporting an offence or giving rise to apprehension for the safety of person or property, or that one has information material to a police enquiry is a summary offence in England under s. 5(2) of the Criminal Law Act 1967.

1-40   It is not, however, a breach of the peace merely to sniff glue while in such a state of intoxication as to be oblivious of one's surroundings: *Fisher* v. *Keane*, 1981 J.C. 50.

Add new paragraph **1-40a**:

1-40a   *Malicious mischief.* In *H.M. Advocate* v. *Wilson*, 1984 S.L.T. 117 it was held that the crime of malicious mischief was not limited to causing physical damage to corporeal property, but extended to cases where loss was caused without any such damage. In that case a generator had been stopped by the pressing of a switch, causing a loss of electricity which cost well over £100,000 to replace: see commentary at 1983 S.C.C.R. 420.

CHAPTER 2

THE CONCEPT OF RESPONSIBILITY

2-09   See Andrew Ashworth, *Sentencing and Penal Policy* (London, 1983) for a general review of recent sentencing theory and practice.

2-11   See D.J. Galligan, "The Return to Retribution in Penal Theory", in *Crime, Proof and Punishment*, ed. Tapper (London, 1981), 144.

2-14   See also N.D. Walker, "The Efficiency and Morality of Deterrents" [1979] Crim. L.R. 129; "Punishing, Denouncing or Reducing Crime", in *Reshaping the Criminal Law*, ed. Glazebrook (London, 1978), 391; "The Ultimate Justification", in *Crime, Proof and Punishment*, ed. Tapper (London, 1981), 109.

2-17   See also *Kiely* v. *Lunn*, 1982 S.C.C.R. 436. *Brennan* v. *H.M.A.* is now reported at 1977 J.C. 38.

CHAPTER 3

THE CRIMINAL ACT

3-02   In *Niven* v. *Tudhope*, 1982 S.C.C.R. 365 a conviction for indecent exposure was quashed because of the absence of any finding of "wilful conduct."

3-10   See also *The Queen* v. *O'Connor* (1980) 54 A.L.J.R. 349.

3-16   To be classed as automatic, behaviour must be wholly unconscious, and a person who acts when his consciousness is merely clouded, is not acting automatically: *Roberts* v. *Ramsbottom* [1980] 1 W.L.R. 823. Behaviour which is purposive cannot count as automatic behaviour: *R.* v. *Isitt* [1977] 67 Cr. App. R.44, where the accused drove off after an accident and engaged in manoeuvres designed to escape from pursuing police officers while he was in a fugue and his mind was shut to moral inhibitions.

3-18   In *R.* v. *Sullivan* [1984] A.C. 156 it was held that automatism could be classed as non-insane where there was temporary impairment not self-induced by drink or drugs but resulting from an external physical factor such as a blow on the head or a medical anaesthetic.

3-19   Epileptic behaviour counts as insanity and not as non-insane automatism in England: *R.* v. *Sullivan* [1984] A.C. 156. See also *R.* v. *Bailey* [1983] 1 W.L.R. 760; *infra*, para. 3-26.

3-20   In a case involving a 14-year-old boy charged with assaulting his five-year-old cousin in which the accused had pled guilty, the Crown agreed to the plea being withdrawn and deserted the diet on receipt of two psychiatric reports expressing the opinion that the boy had been sleep-walking at the relevant time: *H.M.A.* v. *X*, Edinburgh High Court, December 1983, unreported; see *The Scotsman* newspaper, 17th December 1983.

3-21   In *Stirling* v. *Annan*, 1983 S.C.C.R. 396 the Crown conceded that a conviction for shoplifting where the accused was apparently suffering from spontaneous hypoglycaemia might have involved a miscarriage of justice, and the conviction was quashed.

3-23   See also *R.* v. *Bailey* [1983] 1 W.L.R. 760; R.D. Mackay, "Intoxication as a Factor in Automatism" [1982] Crim. L.R. 146. *Brennan* v. *H.M.A.* is now reported at 1977 J.C. 38.

3-26   It was said in *R.* v. *Bailey* [1983] 1 W.L.R. 760 that self-induced automatism could be a defence unless the accused had behaved recklessly. To take drinks or dangerous drugs is always to behave recklessly: *cf. infra*, para. 12-12, but a failure to take food after insulin would not be so unless the accused appreciated that this failure was likely to lead to, *e.g.* violence.
              See also *Roberts* v. *Ramsbottom* [1980] 1 W.L.R. 823.

3-27   See also the approach of the Crown and the High Court in *Stirling* v. *Annan*, 1983 S.C.C.R. 396; *supra*, para. 3-21; and in the case referred to *supra*, para. 3-20.

3-32   *Cf. Fishmongers' Company* v. *Bruce*, 1980 S.L.T. (Notes) 35, 36: "[N]o one can be held guilty of contravening a bye-law which requires that a certain result shall be secured unless he is a person who is charged by the bye-law or by statute with a duty to secure that result."

3-33   In *R.* v. *Miller* [1983] 2 A.C. 161 A was a vagrant who fell asleep smoking a cigarette; the cigarette fell and started a fire. When A woke up the fire was smouldering, but he went away without putting it out. The fire spread and destroyed a building and caused a death. A was convicted of manslaughter and arson. It was said by Lord Diplock that even if one is initially unaware of a train of events which by the time one becomes aware of it obviously creates a risk, one is liable for the consequences if one does not try to prevent or reduce them.

    See also *Jas. Paterson Duff*, Criminal Appeal Court, May 1979, unreported: a charge of culpable homicide by assaulting V to her severe injury and thereafter failing to obtain medical assistance for her, whereby she died as a result of her injuries and the lack of medical attention.

3-38   On the elements needed to prove possession, see *Black* v. *H.M. Advocate*, 1974 J.C. 43.

    Possession requires both knowledge and control, so that mere knowledge on the part of an occupant of a house in multiple occupation that prohibited articles are in the communal livingroom does not amount to possession of them by him: *Mingay* v. *Mackinnon*, 1980 J.C. 33; *cf. Bellerby* v. *Carle* [1983] 2 A.C. 101; *infra*, para. 8-61.

    Footnote 75. *McKenzie* v. *Skeen* is now reported at 1983 S.L.T. 121.

3-39   See Michael Hirst, "Jurisdiction over Cross Border Offences" (1981) 97 L.Q.R. 80.

    Footnote 81. See now Renton & Brown, paras. 1-08 *et seq.*

    Footnote 90. *D.P.P.* v. *Stonehouse* is now reported at [1978] A.C. 55.

3-48   A failure to lodge documents is committed at the place where they should have been lodged: *Smith* v. *Inglis and Ors.*, 1982 S.C.C.R. 403.

3-51   It was held in *Attorney-General's Reference (No. 1 of 1982)* [1983] Q.B. 751 that a conspiracy in England to cause harm to an English company abroad was not indictable in England.

    Special provision is made in section 6 of the Aviation Security Act 1982 for it to be an offence for anyone in the United Kingdom to induce or assist the commission abroad of certain offences under that Act in which the United Kingdom courts have extraterritorial jurisdiction.

3-52   Footnote 30. *D.P.P.* v. *Stonehouse* is now reported at [1978] A.C. 55.

CHAPTER 4

THE PROBLEM OF CAUSATION

4-25   See also *Gizzi and Anr.* v. *Tudhope*, 1982 S.C.C.R. 442.

4-30   See also *Attorney-General's Reference (No. 4 of 1980)* [1981] 1 W.L.R. 705.

4-31   In *The Oropesa* [1943] P. 32, at 39, Lord Wright said, "To break the chain of causation it must be shown that there is something which I will call ultroneous, something unwarrantable, a new cause which disturbs the sequence of events, something which can be described as either unreasonable or extraneous or extrinsic," and this passage was applied in *Finlayson* v. *H.M. Advocate*, 1979 J.C. 33; *infra*, para. 4-33a.

4-33   Add new paragraph **4-33a**:

4-33a   *Life support machines.* In *Finlayson* v. *H.M. Advocate*, 1979 J.C. 33 an injection of a controlled drug caused brain death, but the victim's heart was kept going on a life-support machine. Thereafter it was decided that because there had been brain death the machine should be turned off. At the subsequent trial for culpable homicide of the person who had administered the drug it was argued that death had been caused by the stopping of the machine. It was held that the effects of the drug were the substantial and continuing cause of death which was not affected by the decision to turn off the machine which was in the circumstances a reasonable one. "It follows accordingly that the act of disconnecting the machine can hardly be described as an extraneous or extrinsic act [in terms of Lord Wright's speech in *The Oropesa* [1943] P. 32] . . . Far less can it be said that [it] was either unforeseeable or unforeseen": L.J.G. at 36. No special point was made of the fact that the victim was, in one sense at least, already dead before he was put on the machine, although it was said that the machine was used only to obtain time to ascertain if there was any chance of restoring brain function: See also *R.* v. *Malcherek* [1981] 1 W.L.R. 690; Watson, Harland and MacLean, "Brain Stem Death" (1978) 23 J.L.S. 433; P.D.G. Skegg, "Termination of Life Support and the Law of Murder etc." (1978) 41 M.L.R. 423.

4-42   Footnote 92. It has been held in England that neither an act of self-defence nor an act done in the execution of a public duty is a *novus actus interveniens*. Where, therefore, A tries to prevent his arrest by holding B in front of him as a shield and firing at approaching police officers as a result of which they fire back and kill B, B's death is caused by A's acts, and the action of the police does not break the causal chain: *R.* v. *Pagett* (1983) 76 Cr. App. R. 279. The court's view was that the position would have been the same if A had done no more than use B as a shield and had not himself shot at the police, assuming that the conduct of the latter was within the reasonable execution of their duty.

4-52   It was said in *Ex p. Minister of Justice, Re S.* v. *Grotjohn*, 1970 (2) S.A. 355 (A.D.) that whether or not there is homicide is a question of fact. The court declined to approve a general doctrine that a final voluntary act by the victim would always lead to the acquittal of the accused "without some reservation in regard to the independence of the act." Where the two acts were not totally unconnected, and especially where the result was an eventuality which the perpetrator foresaw as a possibility which he wanted to employ to attain his object

4-52   (the death of the suicide), or as something on which he could depend to bring about the desired result, "it would be contrary to accepted principles of law and to all sense of justice to allow him to take shelter behind the act as a *novus actus interveniens.*" In *Grotjohn* the accused had had a row with his wife who threatened to shoot herself, whereupon he had loaded a rifle and given it to her, saying, "Shoot yourself if you want to, because you're a nuisance," and had been acquitted. The Minister of Justice then referred the case to the court.

In *S. v. Hibbert*, 1979 (4) S.A. 717 (D. and C.L.D.) the facts were much the same, and the accused was convicted on the ground that he must have appreciated the possibility of serious injury and death, and therefore had the necessary intention to murder, and so was reckless as to the consequences of his conduct. Shearer J. said, ". . . the act of pulling the trigger to which all the other conduct conduced, cannot in any sense be described as independent of the course of conduct," so that there was no *novus actus.*

See also D.J. Lanham, "Murder by Instigating Suicide" [1980] Crim. L.R. 215.

4-53   In *Khaliq* v. *H.M. Advocate*, 1984 S.L.T. 137 the accused were charged with supplying children with glue and with containers from which the glue could be sniffed, a combination known as a "glue-sniffing kit," in the knowledge that the children intended to sniff the glue to the danger of their lives and health, and with endangering their lives and health. It was held that the supply of the kits to, and the glue-sniffing by, the children were so closely connected as to be equivalent to the administration of the glue to the children, even in the absence of any averment of instigation, and that the charge was relevant. It was observed that although the age of the sniffers was relevant in considering whether the facts amounted to administration, it was not essential to the relevancy of the charge.

CHAPTER 5

ART AND PART

5-01   Art and part guilt requires involvement in a specific crime, of which each plotter is guilty. It may be, however, that where A is a member of a gang and is sent out to do "a job" without being told specifically what that job involves, he will be guilty of whatever crime is actually committed, provided it is within the range of activities which could reasonably be expected to be carried out by the gang in the circumstances. So, where a terrorist assists in an attack on a target without knowing whether guns or explosives are to be used and in fact explosives are used, he may be guilty art and part of possessing and using explosives, although his own involvement was only to guide the bombers to the scene of the crime and he drove off without seeing any explosives: *R. v. Maxwell* [1978] 1 W.L.R. 1350.

5-02   A person who is not himself related to the parties may be art and part guilty of incest: *Vaughan* v. *H.M.A.*, 1979 S.L.T. 49.

5-02 Footnote 4. See now *H.M.A.* v. *Duffy*, 1983 S.L.T. 7; *infra*, para. 33-12.

5-05 Section 9 of the Sexual Offences (Scotland) Act 1956 is repealed by the Criminal Justice (Scotland) Act 1980: see *infra*, para. 36-17.

5-06 Footnote 22. *R.* v. *Whitehouse* is now reported at [1977] Q.B. 868.

5-10 The Incest Act 1567 can be contravened by a person not related to the persons participating in the unlawful intercourse: *Vaughan* v. *H.M.A.*, 1979 S.L.T. 49. See also *Skinner* v. *Patience and Cowe*, 1982 S.L.T. (Sh. Ct.) 81.

5-11 In *Fishmongers Company* v. *Bruce*, 1980 S.L.T. (Notes) 35 it was held that the person locally in charge of a fishery could not be convicted of breach of a statutory duty in failing to remove the leaders of nets during the weekly close season because the duty of removal was placed only on the proprietor or occupier of the fishery by s. 24 of the Salmon Fisheries (Scotland) Act 1868. The decision proceeded on the basis that the offence was one of omission and could therefore be committed only by someone specifically charged with the relevant duty: see *supra*, para. 3-32; the sheriff thought that an act of commission in breach of the statutory bye-law could be committed by anyone.

5-12 In *Valentine* v. *Mackie*, 1980 S.L.T. (Sh. Ct.) 122 a passenger was convicted of aiding and abetting the driver to drive with an excess of alcohol in his blood: see *infra*, para. 8-37.

5-15 See also *Vaughan* v. *H.M.A.*, 1979 S.L.T. 49.

5-22 For a modern example of art and part by instigation, see *Little* v. *H.M.A.*, 1983 S.C.C.R. 56.

5-27 See also *R.* v. *Maxwell* [1978] 1 W.L.R. 1350; *supra* para. 5-01.

5-35 Where the accused's presence was wholly passive and the Crown are therefore forced to rely on prior concert the jury must be specifically and forcefully directed on the point: *Spiers* v. *H.M.A.*, 1980 J.C. 36.

A senior police officer who fails to interfere when a junior officer assaults a prisoner whom they are both escorting may be art and part guilty of the assault: *Bonar* v. *McLeod*, 1983 S.C.C.R. 161.

5-38 Footnote 6. In *Melvin* v. *H.M. Advocate*, 1984 S.C.C.R. 113 A and B were charged with robbery and murder, and A was convicted of murder and B of culpable homicide. In dismissing A's appeal on the ground that the verdicts were inconsistent, Lord Cameron said at page 117:

> "In determining the quality of the crime, i.e., as between culpable homicide and murder, a jury would be entitled, in a case where intent to kill was not suggested or established or indeed any antecedent concerted intention to carry out an assault and robbery on the deceased or any other

person, to consider and assess the degree of recklessness displayed by each participant and return, if their judgment so required, a discriminating verdict in accordance with their assessment":

See also *Johns* v. *The Queen* (1980) 54 A.L.J.R. 166.

5-39   In *Boyne* v. *H.M. Advocate*, 1980 S.L.T. 56 the victim of an assault and robbery committed by a number of people was killed by one of them with a knife. It was held that the others could be convicted of murder only if they knew that the assailant was carrying a knife at the time and was liable to use it, or if they carried on with the attack on the victim after the knife had been used. The Lord Justice-Clerk said, at page 59:

> "For instance, if an accused was one of a gang who attacked a victim, and says in a statement that he saw another member of the gang, he cannot say who, unexpectedly take out a knife and deliver a blow with it which proved fatal, but nonetheless he carried on with the attack on the victim, we do not see how that statement would not be competent evidence against him on a charge of murder art and part.
>
> Having considered the statements made by Boyne which were properly before the jury and which they manifestly accepted, we are satisfied that there is nothing in them which can be read or interpreted as an admission that he either knew or had reasonable cause to anticipate that Curley might use a knife on the victim or that he, Boyne, carried on with the assault on the victim after Curley had used the knife. The advocate-depute suggested that the inference might be drawn from the statements that Boyne knew that Curley was likely to be carrying a knife on this occasion and was liable to use it. This stemmed from admissions by Boyne that he had seen Curley with a knife on previous occasions. These statements were qualified by assertions: (1) that Curley had told him that he only carried the knife in self-defence, having himself been attacked on a previous occasion; and (2) that while he had been involved with Curley in previous muggings he had never seen Curley use a knife. We reject the advocate-depute's suggestion and hold that there was nothing in Boyne's statements to constitute an acknowledgement that he was art and part in the murder (as distinct from an assault and robbery). The Crown accepted that if that were so there was not sufficient evidence to warrant the conviction of murder in his case. We shall accordingly quash that conviction."

5-46   In *R.* v. *Nathan* [1981] 2 N.Z.L.R. 473 the victim was attacked by a gang who kicked him and hit him with a weapon, but death was probably caused by a minor blow. It was held that since it was not possible to isolate the fatal blow or infer that it was delivered by someone with the requisite knowledge, the members of the gang were all guilty only of manslaughter: *cf. Ramnath Mohan* v. *The Queen* [1967] 2 A.C. 187; *Boyne* v. *H.M.A.*, 1980 S.L.T. 56; *supra*, para. 5.39.

CHAPTER 6

INCHOATE CRIMES

6–15   English law is now governed by the Criminal Attempts Act 1981, section 1 of which provides: "If, with intent to commit an [indictable offence], a person does an act which is more than merely preparatory

6-15   to the commission of the offence, he is guilty of [attempt]." Similar provision is made by s. 3 of the Act for attempts under special statutory provision.

6-19   This theory appears now to be the law of England: Criminal Attempts Act 1981, ss. 1 and 3; *supra.* para. 6-15.

6-21   Footnote 69. Add: *Cf. R.* v. *Matthews* [1981] Crim. L.R. 325.

6-49   Footnote 59. See also Law Commission Report on Attempt and Impossibility in relation to Attempt, Conspiracy and Incitement (Law. Com. No. 102, 1980); H.L.A. Hart, "The House of Lords on attempting the impossible," in *Crime, Proof and Punishment*, ed. Tapper (London, 1981), 1.

6-51   The Criminal Attempts Act 1981 provides that in England a person may be guilty of attempt even though the facts are such that the commission of the offence is impossible, and further that where a person's intention would constitute an intention to commit an offence only if the facts had been as he believed them, he shall be regarded as having such an intention: ss. 1(2),(3) and 3(4),(5). Factual impossibility thus no longer prevents conviction for attempt in England, but the position of legal impossibility is not so clear.

Footnote 69. It was held in *R.* v. *Taaffe* [1984] 2 W.L.R. 326 that a person who imports what he mistakenly believes to be currency in the mistaken belief that its import is prohibited is not "knowingly concerned in any fraudulent evasion" of an import prohibition, although the goods imported were in fact the subject of a prohibition, being prohibited drugs. The question of attempt was not raised.

6-53   It is a crime to attempt to bribe a public official even if the purpose of the bribe is to persuade him to do something which he has no power to do: *Maxwell* v. *H.M.A.*, 1980 J.C. 40; the position in that case was, however, simplified by the fact that bribery is complete when the bribe is offered, whatever follows thereafter: *ibid.; cf. infra*, para. 44-08.

6-55   Conspiracy "is constituted by the agreement of two or more persons to further or achieve a criminal purpose. A criminal purpose is one which if attempted or achieved by action on the part of an individual would itself constitute a crime by the law of Scotland": *Maxwell* v. *H.M.A.*, 1980 J.C. 40, Lord Cameron at 43. See also *Sayers and Ors.* v. *H.M.A.*, 1981 S.C.C.R. 312.

6-63   Lord Cameron's definition of conspiracy in *Maxwell* v. *H.M. Advocate*, 1980 J.C. 40 clearly requires the conspiracy to involve conduct which would be criminal if committed by one person: see *supra*, para. 6-55.

6-67   Add new paragraph **6-67a**:

6-67a   IMPOSSIBILITY. In *Maxwell* v. *H.M. Advocate*, 1980 J.C. 40 the accused were convicted of conspiracy to bribe members of a licensing board to transfer a gaming licence. They appealed on the ground that the conspiracy was incapable of success since at the relevant time the transfer of gaming licences was a matter for the sheriff and not for the licensing board. The appeal failed. Lord Cameron said that a conspiracy was an agreement to achieve a criminal purpose, and that it was the criminality of the purpose and not the result which made the agreement criminal. A conspiracy whose purpose was to corrupt public officials was therefore criminal, whether or not it could have the desired result. This seems, with respect, an odd use of "purpose": the purpose was to get the licence transferred; bribery was the means of effecting that purpose. But, semantics aside, there was clearly a conspiracy to achieve the desired result by criminal means, and there is no question that the means proposed were criminal, and no question of error or impossibility in so far as the intention of giving bribes to public officials was concerned. The case is therefore distinguishable from, *e.g.* a conspiracy to abort a non-pregnant woman, or obtain a passport by arranging a bigamous marriage where the parties in question are in fact, unknown to the conspirators, free to marry. Lord Cameron distinguished the English case of *D.P.P.* v. *Nock* [1978] A.C. 979 where the House of Lords held that it was not a criminal conspiracy to conspire to produce cocaine from a powder from which such production was in fact impossible. There is no reason why that should not be a criminal conspiracy in Scotland by analogy with attempted theft from an empty pocket: para. 6-53 in the main work, and this seems to have been accepted in *Maxwell*: see Lord Cameron at 44-45. It is now a criminal conspiracy in England: Criminal Attempts Act 1981, s. 5.

6-68   There is no case law on incitement to commit the impossible, but the law is doubtless the same as for conspiracy: *supra*, para. 6-67a. The position is different in England because the Criminal Attempts Act 1981 does not apply to incitement: *R.* v. *Fitzmaurice* [1983] Q.B. 1083; see also M. Cohen, "Inciting the Impossible" [1979] Crim.L.R. 239.

CHAPTER 7

THE CRIMINAL MIND

7-13   Footnote 35. See also Law Commission Report on the Mental Element in Crime (Law Com. No. 89, 1978), and articles thereon in [1978] Crim.L.R. 588; R.A. Duff, "Intention, Mens Rea and the Law Commission's Report" [1980] Crim.L.R. 147; "Intention, Recklessness and Probable Consequences", *ibid.* 404; "Recklessness", *ibid.* 282; see also Scottish Law Commission's Report on the Mental Element in Crime (Scot. Law Com. No. 80, 1983).

7-14   Asquith L.J.'s definition was adopted by the trial judge in *Sayers and Ors.* v. *H.M. Advocate*, 1981 S.C.C.R. 312.

7-18   See also *R.* v. *Lemon* [1979] A.C. 617, especially Lord Diplock at 634E-F; *R.* v. *Maxwell* [1978] 1 W.L.R. 1350.

7-34   It is now the law of England that "wilful" in the context of wilful neglect means intentional or reckless: *R.* v. *Sheppard* [1981] A.C. 394. Neglect to maintain one's dependants is something different again: see *Galt* v. *Turner*, 1981 S.C.C.R. 111.

7-35   Footnote 11. Add: D. Calligan, "Responsibility for Recklessness" (1978) 31 Curr. Leg. Problems 55; R.A. Duff, "Recklessness" [1980] Crim.L.R. 282.

7-52   *Cf.* Lord Diplock in *R.* v. *Sheppard* [1981] A.C. 394, 404 A-B:

> "The concept of the reasonable man as providing the standard by which the liability of real persons for their actual conduct is to be determined is a concept of civil law, particularly in relation to the tort of negligence; the obtrusion into criminal law of conformity with the notional conduct of the reasonable man as relevant to criminal liability, though not unknown (e.g., in relation to provocation sufficient to reduce murder to manslaughter), is exceptional, and should not lightly be extended: *Andrews* v. *Director of Public Prosecutions* [1937] A.C. 576, 582-583. If failure to use the hypothetical powers of observation, ratiocination and foresight of consequences possessed by this admirable but purely notional exemplar is to constitute an ingredient of a criminal offence it must surely form part not of the actus reus but of the mens rea."

7-56   In *The Queen* v. *O'Connor* (1980) 54 A.L.J.R. 349, Barwick C.J. at 355, discussing the rule that self-induced intoxication is not a defence (see *infra*, para. 12-12) said: "A distrust of jurors and an anxiety that they may too readily be persuaded to an acquittal if evidence of the result of self-induced intoxication, particularly by drugs other than alcohol, were allowed, may have formed some part of the public policy on which the decision rests." He then quoted the trial judge, Starke J., as saying, "I, of course. have no knowledge of how English juries react . . . I do not share the fear held by many in England that if intoxication is accepted as a defence as far as general intent is concerned the floodgates will open and hordes of guilty men will descend on the community".

7-57
to   See *infra*, paras. 7-70 to 7-74.
7-61

7-67   See *People* v. *Murray* [1977] I.R.360: advertent recklessness as to whether victim a police officer sufficient for capital murder requiring intention to kill or cause serious injury to a police officer.

7-70   It is now clear that recklessness in Scots law is basically objective,
to   and that in both Scots and English law a person who gives no thought to
7-74   a risk may be reckless: *Allan* v. *Patterson*, 1980 J.C. 57; *R.* v. *Caldwell* [1982] A.C. 341; *R.* v. *Lawrence (Stephen)* [1982] A.C. 510; *Elliott* v. *C.* [1983] 1 W.L.R. 939. For criticisms of the English decisions see, *e.g.* Professors J.C. Smith and Glanville Williams in [1981] Crim. L.R. 392,

7-70
to
7-74
580, 658; E. Griew, "Reckless Damage and Reckless Driving", *ibid.*
743; Glanville Williams, "Recklessness Redefined", 1981 C.L.J. 252;
R.A. Duff, "Professor Williams and Conditional Subjectivism", *ibid.*,
273; G. Syrota, "A Radical Change in the Law of Recklessness" [1982]
Crim. L.R. 97. On the apparently special position of rape, see *R.* v.
Satnam S. (1984) 78 Cr. App.R. 149.

In *Allan* v. *Patterson*, which was a charge of reckless driving contrary
to s. 2 of the Road Traffic Act 1972 which simply makes it an offence to
drive recklessly, Lord Justice-General Emslie said, at page 60:

> "There is nothing in the language of section 2 as amended to suggest an
> intention on the part of Parliament to penalise thereunder only a course of
> driving embarked upon wilfully or deliberately in the face of known risks
> of a material kind. Inquiry into the state of knowledge of a particular
> driver accused of the offence created by the section as amended, and into
> his intention at the time, is not required at all. The statute directs
> attention to the quality of the driving in fact but not to the state of mind or
> the intention of the driver. If it were otherwise, the section, and indeed
> section 1, would virtually become inoperable in all but the rarest of
> instances."

Cf. Peda v. *The Queen* [1969] S.C.R. 905.

That, of course, was said in the context of a statutory offence, and
even in that context may overstate the irrelevance of the driver's
knowledge of the situation with which he was faced. But the case was
argued by the Crown on the basis of the ordinary meaning of the word
"reckless" as an adverb qualifying "drives." "Recklessness", in other
words, describes behaviour rather than a state of mind; and it can
therefore be satisfied by a blank state of mind.

Allan v. *Patterson* has since been explicitly applied to the reckless
discharge of firearms, a common law offence, in *Gizzi and Anr.* v.
Tudhope, 1982 S.C.C.R. 442. In that case the firearms were discharged in ignorance of the presence of persons working behind some
trees. The accused were convicted because they had done little or
nothing to satisfy themselves that no one was within range: see also *W.*
v. *H.M. Advocate*, 1982 S.C.C.R. 152.

It is also clear from the above cases that the degree of risk which is
ignored, or to which the accused is "utterly indifferent", must be very
high, and indeed the main question in the appeal in *Gizzi* was whether
the risk had been shown to be sufficiently great, or sufficiently obvious
to the reasonable man, to raise the accuseds' conduct from negligence
to recklessness.

CHAPTER 8

MENS REA IN STATUTORY OFFENCES

8-05
On the general question of *mens rea* or strict liability, see *Beaver* v.
The Queen [1957] S.C.R. 531; *The Queen* v. *Sault Ste Marie* [1978] 2
S.C.R. 1299; *infra*, para. 8-33.

8-07
Footnote 29. Add: Hallmarking Act 1973, s. 1; *Chilvers* v. *Rayne*
[1984] 1 W.L.R. 328.

8-14   *Alphacell* was followed in *Lockhart* v. *N.C.B.*, 1981 S.L.T. 161; *infra*, para. 8-29.

8-15   See, *e.g. MacNeill* v. *Wilson*, 1981 S.C.C.R. 80; use of vehicle with dangerous load.

8-21   Footnote 94. *R.* v. *Manners-Astley* was overruled by the House of Lords in *R.* v. *Terry* [1984] 2 W.L.R. 23, which held that "fraudulently" includes an intent to deceive a public official into doing or refraining from something he would not otherwise have done or refrained from doing.

8-23   In *Sutherland* v. *Aitchison*, 1975 J.C. 1, another case of failing to stop after an accident, the driver heard a bump as he squeezed past another car on a single track road. He thought the bump was caused by his exhaust hitting a stone and drove on. It was held that, having heard the bump, it was his duty to stop and see if there had been an accident. Where, therefore, something happens which should alert the accused to the possibility that the circumstances may be such as to require him to do something, he is not entitled to act on a belief that these circumstances do not exist, but is bound to make inquiry.

8-25   See also *Bellerby* v. *Carle* [1983] 2 A.C. 101, *infra*, para. 8-61.

8-27   Footnote 37. *Brennan* v. *H.M.A.* is now reported at 1977 J.C. 38.

8-29   See M. Budd and A. Lynch, "Voluntariness, Causation and Strict Liability" [1978] Crim. L.R. 74.
     Alphacell Ltd. v. *Woodward* was followed in *Lockhart* v. *N.C.B.*, 1981 S.L.T. 161 where the accused were convicted of causing polluting matter to enter a river from a mine which they had ceased to occupy, so that they were no longer able to carry out the pumping operations necessary to prevent the pollution: see *infra*, para. 8-69.

     Add new paragraph **8-29a**:

8-29a   *Necessity and coercion.* Since these pleas are effective even when the accused acts freely and knowingly, and since they depend on the objective circumstances rather than on the accused's state of mind (see Chap. 13 in the main work), they are applicable to offences of strict responsibility. In *Tudhope* v. *Grubb*, 1983 S.C.C.R. 350 (Sh. Ct.) the defence of necessity was upheld where the accused who had an excess of alcohol in his blood tried to drive his car in order to escape from an assault.

8-33   In *The Queen* v. *Sault Ste Marie* [1978] 2 S.C.R. 1299 the Canadian Supreme Court divided offences into three categories:— those requiring *mens rea*; strict liability offences, in which *mens rea* need not be established but the defence of reasonable care or reasonable mistake is available; and absolute liability offences in which the accused cannot exculpate himself by showing he was free of fault; and held that public welfare offences were to be regarded as offences of strict liability unless the legislature clearly made them offences of absolute liability.

8-33 Footnote 73. *Lambie* v. *H.M.A.* is now reported at 1973 J.C. 53.

8-37 In *Valentine* v. *Mackie*, 1980 S.L.T. (Sh. Ct.) 122 A was convicted of aiding and abetting the driver of the car in which he was a passenger to drive with an excess of alcohol in his blood, on the basis that, given that they had been drinking together and the car was being driven erratically, a reasonable man in A's position would have realised that the driver was likely to be over the limit; following *Carter* v. *Richardson* [1974] R.T.R. 314. A was the owner of the car and was acting as supervisor of the driver who held a provisional licence.

8-46 See also *Skinner* v. *MacLean*, 1979 S.L.T. (Notes) 35.

8-47 It has been said in England that "use" by a passenger is limited to employers or to cases where the vehicle is being used directly for the accused's own purposes: *Bennett* v. *Richardson* [1980] R.T.R. 358. See also *Passmoor* v. *Gibbons* [1979] R.T.R. 53.

Where a group of people act together in stealing or unlawfully taking a vehicle, they are all treated as using the vehicle: *cf. Leathley* v. *Tatton* [1980] R.T.R. 21.

On the other hand, where a passenger becomes aware in the course of a journey that the car has been unlawfully taken and that the driver is therefore uninsured, he does not become a user by remaining in the car, and indeed he may not be a user even if he knows the position before he accepts a lift, albeit he will be guilty of allowing himself to be carried in an unlawfully taken vehicle: see *B (A Minor)* v. *Knight* [1981] R.T.R. 136.

Footnote 46. *Swan* v. *MacNab* is now reported at 1977 J.C. 57.

8-56 But see *Bellerby* v. *Carle* [1983] 2 A.C. 101; *infra*, para. 8-61, which requires a degree of personal control.

8-59 See also *Byrne* v. *Tudhope*, 1983 S.C.C.R. 337.

8-61 The fact that a licensee is the only person who can lawfully use liquid measures for the sale of liquor does not in itself mean that he is in possession of them for the purpose of the offence of possessing unjust measures, contrary to the Weights and Measures Act 1963, s. 16; he must be shown to have a degree of control over them: *Bellerby* v. *Carle* [1983] 2 A.C. 101. The House of Lords seem to have been influenced by the fact that section 16 creates offences of using and possessing unjust weights, but provides a defence of lack of knowledge only in relation to use, making possession an offence of strict responsibility.

See also *MacDonald* v. *Smith*, 1979 J.C. 55; *Sopp* v. *Long* [1970] 1 Q.B. 518.

8-69 Where an offence of causing something to occur is strict, it is no defence that the forbidden result occurred because of a failure by someone else to take precautions, or that the accused was no longer in a position to prevent the result. In *Lockhart* v. *N.C.B.*, 1981 S.L.T. 161, the Coal Board were convicted of causing polluting matter to enter a river from disused workings which had some time before

8-69   passed out of their control into that of someone else who had not kept up the precautions taken by the Board when they had been in occupation. It was held that as the Board had set up a system under which pollution was bound to occur in the absence of preventive measures they had caused the pollution. The only defences which might be open were acts of a third party or act of God; the mere fact that the accused could no longer legally enter the mine to take the necessary precautions was irrelevant. The High Court in this case accepted *Alphacell Ltd.* v. *Woodward* [1972] A.C. 824 as representing Scots law.

8-70   Footnote 39a. *Swan* v. *MacNab* is now reported at 1977 J.C. 57.

8-72   Footnote 44. *Smith of Maddiston Ltd.* v. *MacNab* is now reported at 1975 J.C. 48.

8-74   The "ought to have known" criterion was applied in *MacPhail* v. *Allan and Dey Ltd.*, 1980 S.L.T. (Sh. Ct.) 136 where the accused company's transport manager had no system for checking whether drivers had valid licences.

8-75   Add new paragraph **8-75a**:

8-75a   *Driving licences.* It was held in *Ferrymasters Ltd* v. *Adams* [1980] R.T.R. 139 that the offence of causing or permitting someone to drive without a licence was in the same position as that of causing or permitting someone to drive uninsured. In *MacPhail* v. *Allan and Dey Ltd.*, 1980 S.L.T. (Sh. Ct.) 136 the sheriff refused to follow that decision, holding it be inconsistent with *Smith of Maddiston Ltd.* v. *MacNab*, 1975 J.C. 48.

8-79   See *Dean* v. *John Menzies (Holdings) Ltd.*, 1981 J.C. 23, Lord Maxwell at 40-41.

8-80   See also *MacPhail* v. *Allan and Dey Ltd.*, 1980 S.L.T. (Sh. Ct.) 136; *supra*, para. 8-64. *Smith of Maddiston Ltd.* v. *MacNab* is now reported at 1975 J.C. 48.

8-84 to 8-90   There is now a decision of the Criminal Appeal Court on the responsibility of a company for a common law crime, *Dean* v. *John Menzies (Holdings) Ltd.*, 1981 J.C. 23 (see Steven L. Stuart, "The Case of the Shameless Company" (1981) 26 J.L.S. 176 and 222), but it does not make the law entirely clear. This is partly because the crime involved was the new form of shameless indecency which consists in selling obscene articles. Lord Cameron, who was prominent in the development of this crime (see *supra*, para. 1-32; *infra*, para. 41-16), held that it could be committed by a company, but the majority of the court (Lord Stott and Lord Maxwell, who had not been in the earlier obscenity cases and some of whose comments suggest less than enthusiasm for them) held that a company could not be guilty of shameless indecency. The result is that while an individual who knowingly sells obscene books may be convicted of shameless indecency, a label carrying strongly stigmatic overtones, a limited company which is in business solely for the purpose of selling such materials can be convicted only of a contravention of the Civic Government (Scotland) Act 1982: its shop managers may be shamelessly indecent; it may not. If the company had been charged under the then applicable local statute it would have had no argument on the competency of the offence. But the Crown, having chosen instead to use their new toy, were hoist with their own petard. Shameless indecency connotes certain human characteristics and therefore cannot be committed by a company, and it does not matter that none of its original human characteristics is present when it takes the form of selling obscene magazines.

The result is that the incompetency of charging a company with an offence is limited to offences involving peculiarly human characteristics such as shame.

In *Dean* v. *John Menzies Holdings Ltd.*, the majority declined to answer the general question whether a company can commit a common law crime, but Lord Stott said, at p.35:

> "It is I think self-evident that there are certain crimes and offences which cannot be committed by a corporate body. Murder is such a crime, not only, as the Advocate-Depute conceded, because a company cannot be imprisoned but because it is incapable of having that wicked intent or recklessness of mind necessary to constitute the crime of murder. Other examples which come to mind are reset and perjury. In my opinion the offence of conducting oneself in a shamelessly indecent manner falls into the same category."

That a company cannot commit perjury is due to the fact that it cannot be put on oath, but it is difficult to see why a company which has a policy of buying stolen goods should not be guilty of reset. Nor is it easy to see why a company should not be guilty of conspiracy to commit any crime. Lord Stott conceded that a company was capable of some degree of criminal intent, including an intent to deceive, and he accepted *D.P.P.* v. *Kent and Sussex Contractors* [1944] K.B. 146. It seems, therefore, that there are some kinds of intention which a company is capable of having, and others which it cannot have. It can be greedy, but it cannot harbour thoughts of violence; and it has no shame and no lustful thoughts.

Lord Maxwell was less inclined to admit the possibility of any form of common law *mens rea* in the case of a company than was Lord Stott. He regarded any attribution of *mens rea* to a company as necessarily a fiction, since a corporation is an abstraction. His Lordship said at p.39:

> "Whatever may be the position as regards other common law crimes, it is perfectly apparent that the company as a legal abstraction could not, as matter of fact, have the knowledge, exercise the judgment and conduct itself in the manner alleged in the complaint. Accordingly the complaint can only become competent by the employment of a fiction (*Tesco* per Lord Reid). Fiction has frequently been employed both in England and Scotland to attribute to a corporation human characteristics which it cannot have, but the fiction which has been employed is not always the same fiction. It seems to me that the approach of the Courts has been this. Where the plain requirements of justice, the express provisions of statute, or the presumed intentions of Parliament require human characteristics to be attributed to corporations the courts provide the necessary fictions tailored to give effect to those requirements, provisions, or intentions."

As examples his Lordship referred to *Clydebank Co-operative Ltd.* v. *Binnie*, 1937 J.C. 17 and *Mackay Brothers* v. *Gibb*, 1969 J.C. 26 as involving different fictions from that of the controlling mind as discussed in *Tesco Supermarkets Ltd* v. *Nattrass* [1972] A.C. 153: for a discussion of these cases see para. 8-90 in the main work. (His Lordship seems to have regarded all corporate responsibility as a form of vicarious responsibility, and so to have rejected any specific distinction between responsibility for offences which do and those which do not involve vicarious responsibility: his view seems to be that each offence has to be looked at separately to determine whether and if so in what manner responsibility can be attributed to a corporation.) His Lordship concluded, at p.45:

> "In the light of the authorities cited to us I am not satisfied that the common law of Scotland recognises any clear single fiction which would, for purposes of criminal responsibility, in all matters attribute to a company the kind of human characteristics and conduct alleged in this complaint. It appears to me unrealistic to suggest that the accused company will be guilty if, but only if, some individuals or individual, whose status is not precisely defined, but who must be vaguely at or near director level, had knowledge of the contents of the magazines in question and acted in a shameless and indecent manner in deciding to sell them. That, however, seems to me to be the result of applying the controlling mind fiction. If some other fiction is to be applied I do not know what it is. I accordingly consider that the complaint here is incompetent. It may be that the criminal law of England would reach a different result (*R.* v. *I.C.R. Haulage Limited* [1944] K.B. 551). If so, it would not be the first time."

Lord Cameron, who would have upheld the competency of the charge, stressed that it concerned matters which were within the power of the company — sales in the course of its business, and this certainly seems a necessary limitation on corporate responsibility. His Lordship accepted *Tesco Supermarkets Ltd.* [1972] A.C. 153 and *Lennard's Carrying Co.* v. *Asiatic Petroleum Co. Ltd.* [1915] A.C. 705 as applicable in Scots law. On the specific question of shamelessness, Lord Cameron's view was that shamelessness in this particular offence was an objective matter which did not involve moral obloquy. His Lordship said, at p.32:

> "The question is not whether a company is an entity which is endowed with a conscience to be appeased or a capacity for moral sensation or an absence of a sense of shame or even a capacity to overcome a sense of shame by the prospect of financial profit. It may well be that the offence libelled is one which falls within the category of offences against public morals, but in order to commit it the offender does not require to be possessed of capacity to feel a sense of personal shame or even to lack it."

Despite the specific reservation by the majority of the general question of corporate responsibility, and despite Lord Cameron's specific acceptance of such responsibility, the likely practical result of *Dean* v. *John Menzies' (Holdings) Ltd.*, particularly in the light of Lord Maxwell's opinion, is that corporations will not be charged with common law offences. There remains, however, much force in Lord Cameron's statement at pp. 28-29 that:

> "The criminal law has long recognised that a corporate body may be guilty

of breaches of statute and incur a penalty, and therefore be susceptible to prosecution as a person recognised in the eyes of the law. Further, the law has also recognised that an incorporation may be guilty of statutory offences the commission of which is the result of intended or deliberate action or inaction. It was not Parliament which specifically provided that corporate bodies such as limited companies should be subject to prosecution: the various statutes assumed that no distinction in capacity to offend should exist between natural and other persons recognised by law as legal entities with capacity to discharge certain functions and perform certain actions. The responsibility of both for breaches of statute is the same, and the individual and the company alike can be cited and charged in their own names . . . If Parliament had intended that a company in its individual capacity should not be liable to prosecution in respect of common law offences it could have said so, and at the same time prescribed where and on what natural persons within the structure or employment of the company responsibility and consequent criminal liability should fall. But Parliament has not so provided, and the authorities cited by the Advocate-Depute illustrate the extent to which companies in Scotland can be and are rendered liable to criminal prosecution, even where commission of the offence libelled involves a conscious exercise of will or demonstration of intent. It would seem therefore to follow that there should be no obstacle in principle to the same liability to prosecution where the offence is *malum in se* and not *malum prohibitum*. This distinction lay at the root of Mr Kerrigan's argument that the question of common law liability was a matter for Parliament and not for the Courts. The fallacy of this argument however would seem to lie in the fact this is not a case of creating or declaring a new crime or offence which never existed before, nor of extending the boundaries of criminal responsibility to a group of legal persons on whose shoulders criminal responsibility had not been rested before. If therefore a limited company has the capacity to form an intention, to decide on a course of action, to act in accordance with that deliberate intent within the scope and limits of its articles, it is difficult to see on what general principle it should not be susceptible to prosecution where that action offends against the common law."

It seems, therefore, that Lord Cameron might have regarded conduct which does involve a sense of shame as beyond the capacity of a corporation, and so as forming an exception, along with offences punishable only custodially or physically, to the general rule of corporate responsibility: see his Lordship's opinion at p.31.

8-90   The applicability of *Tesco Supermarkets Ltd.* v. *Nattrass* [1972] A.C. 153 in Scotland was doubted by Lord Maxwell in *Dean* v. *John Menzies (Holdings) Ltd.*, *supra*, partly on the basis of the Scottish decisions discussed in the main text. *Readers Digest Association Ltd.* v. *Pirie* was distinguished as concerned with a statutory defence.

8-93   Neglect is attributable where the accused has failed to take steps to prevent the commission of an offence by a corporation, if taking these steps falls or should be held to fall within the scope of the functions of his office: *Wotherspoon* v. *H.M. Advocate*, 1978 J.C. 74, L.J-G. at 78.

A local authority director of roads is a "manager, secretary or other similar officer" of the authority: *Armour* v. *Skeen*, 1977 J.C. 15.

CHAPTER 9

ERROR

9-06   On rape, see *infra*, paras. 9-25 to 9-33.

9-12   For a criticism of this section, see J.H. Pain, "Aberratio Ictus. A Comedy of Errors — and Deflection" (1978) 95 S.A.L.J. 480, 482-484.

9-16   It has been held in South Africa that an error of law is no different from an error of fact, so that even an unreasonable error of law will excuse, provided that where the crime is one of negligence there was nothing to put the accused on his guard as to the possibility that his behaviour was illegal: *S. v. De Bloom*, 1977 (3) S.A. 513 (A.D.), where the offence was illegally exporting jewellery; see R.C. Whiting "Changing the Face of Mens Rea" (1978) 95 S.A.L.J. 1. The court's view was that "At this stage of our legal development it must be accepted that the cliché that 'every person is presumed to know the law' has no ground for its existence and that the view that 'ignorance of the law is no excuse' is not legally applicable in the light of the present day concept of mens rea in our law."

In *Secretary of State for Trade and Industry* v. *Hart* [1982] 1 W.L.R. 481 A was charged with acting as a company auditor when he knew he was disqualified by reason of being a director of the company, contrary to section 13(5) of the Companies Act 1976, which provides that "No person shall act as auditor of a company at a time when he knows that he is disqualified . . ." The court held that it was necessary for conviction not merely that the accused knew he was a director, but that he knew that directors were disqualified from acting as auditors. Woolf, J. said, at 485F, "The words in their ordinary interpretation are wholly consistent with a view of the subsections which means that a person in the position of the defendant must be aware of the statutory restrictions which exist against his holding the appointment."

It is not yet clear how far this decision will extend. Woolf, J. referred to the possibility of amending the Act. Ormrod, L.J. said, "If that means that he is entitled to rely on ignorance of the law as a defence, in contrast to the usual practice and the usual rule, the answer is that the section gives him that right. Whether it does so intentionally or not is another matter": at 487-488. His Lordship also referred to the difficulty of proving ignorance, but if the offence requires knowledge it will be for the prosecution to prove knowledge.

It may, therefore, be the law that where a statute requires knowledge of some particular circumstance which involves a rule of law, ignorance of that rule of law is a defence where it leads to lack of the knowledge required by the statute.

9-17   A belief by a property owner that a person who is actually a protected tenant is a squatter may be relevant in a charge of harassment: *R. v. Phekoo* [1981] 1 W.L.R. 1117; but *cf. R. v. Kimber* [1983] 1 W.L.R. 1118.

9-17   Footnote 44. It was held in the Canadian case of *The Queen* v. *Prue* [1979] 2 S.C.R. 547 that as the offence of driving while disqualified was one requiring *mens rea*, it required knowledge of the disqualification, even where the disqualification was an automatic consequence of the accused's earlier convictions. Where, therefore, the accused knew that he had been convicted but had not been told that he was disqualified, he was not guilty of driving while disqualified, his error being treated as one of fact. The case is, however, complicated by reason of the disqualification being the result of provincial legislation while the offence of driving while disqualified is a federal one.

9-21   See also *Tudhope* v. *Lee*, 1982 S.C.C.R. 409 (Sh. Ct.). There are no Scottish cases on entrapment, except in the context of the law of evidence: see *Cook* v. *Skinner*, 1977 J.C. 9. For a general discussion of entrapment, see *Amato* v. *The Queen* [1982] 2 S.C.R. 418.

9-25   These paragraphs must now be read subject to the dictum in *Meek*
to   *and Ors.* v. *H.M. Advocate*, 1982 S.C.C.R. 613 that the Scots courts
9-33   would answer the question in *Morgan* in the same way as did the House of Lords: see the commentary at 1982 S.C.C.R. 620; Peter Ferguson, "Rape and Reasonable Belief", 1983 S.L.T. (News) 89; the Scottish Law Commission do not regard *Meek* as an authority on recklessness — see their Report on the Mental Element in Crime 1983 (Scot. Law Com. No. 80), para. 4.30, n.1.

There have been suggestions in England that *Morgan* is limited to rape, or at least does not apply to certain statutory offences where error to be relevant must be based on reasonable grounds: *R.* v. *Phekoo* [1981] 1 W.L.R. 1117; *Albert* v. *Lavin* [1981] A.C. 546, D.C.; but these cases were doubted in *R.* v. *Kimber* [1983] 1 W.L.R. 1118, where *Morgan* was applied to indecent assault, and it is difficult to see any halfway house between the application of *Morgan* and strict responsibility.

There is specific statutory provision in England that in determining whether or not the man believed the woman was a consenting party the jury may take into account the presence or absence of reasonable grounds for the belief: Sexual Offences (Amendment) Act 1976, s. 1(2). It seems that recklessness in relation to error in rape depends on *Morgan* and on that statutory provision, and is unaffected by later development in the general law of recklessness such as *R.* v. *Caldwell* [1982] A.C. 341; *supra*, paras. 7-70 to 7-74: see *R.* v. *Satnam S.* (1984) 78 Cr. App. R. 312; *cf. R.* v. *Pigg* [1982] 1 W.L.R. 762. Drunken error is irrelevant: *R.* v. *Woods* (1981) 74 Cr. App. R. 312.

On the question of when it is necessary to direct a jury on the defence of belief in consent, see *Meek, supra*, which follows *Morgan* in this too, as does *Pappajohn* v. *The Queen* [1980] 2 S.C.R. 121; see also *R.* v. *Bashir* (1982) 77 Cr. App. R. 59.

It has been held in Australia that a plea of self-defence requires that the accused's belief that he was being attacked in such a way as to justify his retaliation must be reasonable, and is to be judged on the basis of what the accused himself might reasonably believe in the circumstances: *Viro* v. *The Queen* (1976-1978) 141 C.L.R. 88, 146; *R.* v. *Wills* [1983] 2 V.R. 201.

CHAPTER 10

INSANITY

10-01   Footnote 2. *Brennan* v. *H.M.A.* is now reported at 1977 J.C. 38.

10-05   Section 6(2) of the Mental Health (Scotland) Act 1960, inserted by
s. 5 of the Mental Health (Amendment) (Scotland) Act 1983, provides
that no one shall be treated under the Act "as suffering from mental
disorder by reason only of promiscuity or other immoral conduct,
sexual deviancy or dependance on alcohol or drugs." The 1983 Act
also rewrites s. 23 of the 1960 Act, so that no one may be compulsorily
admitted to hospital under section 24 of that Act for mental illness
unless it is appropriate for him to receive medical treatment in a
hospital and it is necessary for his health or safety or the protection of
others that he should receive such treatment and it cannot be provided
unless he is detained: Mental Health (Scotland) Act 1960, s. 23(1), as
substituted by Mental Health (Amendment) (Scotland) Act 1983,
s. 8(1).

10-07   Footnote 19. This should read "1975 Act, ss. 174, 375, 376(3)."

         Footnote 23a. ⎫   *Brennan* v. *H.M.A.* is now reported at 1977
10-22   Footnote 73. ⎭   J.C. 38.

10-40   For an interesting discussion of the difference between appreciation
and knowledge, see *The Queen* v. *Barnier* [1980] 1 S.C.R. 1124.

CHAPTER 11

DIMINISHED RESPONSIBILITY

11-03   See also M. Wasik, "Partial Excuses in Criminal Law" (1982) 45
M.L.R. 516.

         Footnote 20.   ⎫   *Brennan* v. *H.M.A.* is now reported at 1977
11-05   Footnote 30a. ⎭   J.C. 38.

11-06   See also *Duff* v. *H.M. Advocate*, 1983 S.C.C.R. 461.

11-22   Section 6(2) of the Mental Health (Scotland) Act 1960, as inserted
by s. 5 of the Mental Health (Amendment) (Scotland) Act 1983,
provides that no one shall be treated under the Act "as suffering from
mental disorder by reason only of promiscuity or other immoral
conduct, sexual deviancy or dependence on alcohol or drugs."
    The distinction between persons under and persons over 21 is
removed by s. 8(1) of the 1983 Act which rewrites s. 23 of the 1960 Act
so that a hospital order under s. 24 can be made on any person whose

11-22   mental disorder is a persistent one manifested only by abnormally aggressive or seriously irresponsible conduct only where it is appropriate for him to receive medical treatment in a hospital which is likely to alleviate or prevent a deterioration of his condition, and such treatment is necessary for his own health or safety and the protection of others and cannot be provided unless he is detained under the Act. In view of current psychiatric attitudes psychopaths are unlikely to be dealt with under the Act.

11-23   Footnote 15a. *Brennan* v. *H.M.A.* is now reported at 1977 J.C. 38.

11-24   Section 5(1) of the Mental Health (Amendment) (Scotland) Act 1983 replaces the term "mental deficiency" with the term "mental handicap." A person of any age may be compulsorily detained in the same circumstances as any other mentally disordered person, provided the handicap is severe mental impairment, or, where the impairment is not severe, the appropriate treatment "is likely to alleviate or prevent a deterioration of his condition": Mental Health (Scotland) Act 1960, s. 23(1), as substituted by Mental Health (Amendment) (Scotland) Act 1983, s. 8(1).

CHAPTER 12

INTOXICATION

12-01   *Brennan* v. *H.M. Advocate* is now reported at 1977 J.C. 38. See on
et seq. that case J.W.R. Gray, "The Expulsion of Beard from Scotland: Murder North of the Border" [1979] Crim.L.R. 369.

12-12   The Australian High Court by a majority refused to follow *Majewski* in *The Queen* v. *O'Connor* (1980) 54 A.L.J.R. 349, a case of unlawful wounding by a person under the influence of drugs and alcohol. He had stabbed a police officer who was about to arrest him for stealing inter alia the knife involved from the officer's car. The jury had been directed that while intoxication was a relevant defence to the charges of theft and of wounding with intent to resist arrest with which he was indicted, they were not relevant to the offence of unlawful wounding of which they were entitled to convict. Barwick, C.J. said, ". . . proof of a state of intoxication, whether self-induced or not, so far from constituting itself a matter of defence or excuse, is at most merely part of the totality of the evidence which may raise a reasonable doubt as to the existence of essential elements of criminal responsibility": at 351-352; *cf. Kennedy* v. *H.M.A.*, 1944 J.C. 171, L.J-G. at 177; *Leary* v. *The Queen* [1978] 1 S.C.R. 29, Dickson, J. diss. at 43-44. Barwick, C.J. went on to point out that while there are doubtless cases where a person sets out to become intoxicated, there are also cases where "the state of intoxication may be reached by inadvertence, even though the drug . . . may be taken voluntarily", as where a diner "does not observe the frequency with which the waiter tops up his glass", 54 A.L.J.R. at 353, and that *Majewski* (and *a fortiori Brennan*, we might

12-12 add) would apply to such a case. He therefore suggested that if voluntary intoxication is to be a basis of criminal responsibility, a distinction ought to be made between wantonly taking drink or drugs with a view to becoming intoxicated, and cases where such wantonness or indifference is absent. Recklessness was used in *Majewski*, he said, outside its usual use in relation to criminal responsibility: at 355; see also the comments at p. 357. It should, however, be pointed out that Australia (as did England at the time of *Majewski*) adopts a subjective approach to recklessness.

Barwick, C.J. also pointed out that the evidence in *Majewski* did not support a conclusion of involuntariness, and that the House of Lords was not concerned with the voluntariness of Majewski's actings as distinct from their intentional nature: *ibid.* 353-354. It is, however, accepted in Britain that intoxication is irrelevant to automatism, *i.e.* that it cannot exclude voluntariness: *supra*, para. 3-23.

The *O'Connor* approach has now been followed in South Africa in *S. v. Chretien*, 1981 (1) S.A. 1097 (A.D.), rejecting the earlier case of *S. v. Jonson*, 1969 (1) S.A. 201 (A.D.); see J.M. Burchell, "Intoxication and the Criminal Law" (1981) 98 S.A.L.J. 177. The majority of the Canadian Supreme Court preferred *Majewski* in *Leary* v. *The Queen*, *supra*.

12-14 Add new paragraph **12-14a**:

12-14a *Error.* There is no Scots law on the effect of intoxication on the law of error. The English view is that where a statute provides a defence of honest belief, a belief induced by drink is relevant: *Jaggard* v. *Dickinson* [1981] Q.B. 527, but that drunken error does not exclude recklessness: *R.* v. *Woods* (1981) 74 Cr. App. R. 312.

It is possible that Scots law will disregard any error caused by self-induced intoxication, even perhaps one which negatives an esssential part of the definition of the crime, such as a drunken belief that one is taking one's own umbrella.

12-20 Barwick, C.J. suggested in *The Queen* v. *O'Connor* (1980) 54 A.L.J.R. 349, 358, that juries should be entitled to acquit on the ground of intoxication, and to bring in a verdict that the accused had brought on his own irresponsibility, and that such a verdict should make the accused liable to a substantial penalty.

CHAPTER 13

NECESSITY, COERCION AND SUPERIOR ORDERS

13-06 In *Tudhope* v. *Grubb*, 1983 S.C.C.R. 350 (Sh. Ct.) the need to escape assault was accepted as a defence to a charge of attempting to drive with an excess of alcohol in one's blood. The situation was essentially one of self-defence, but the prima facie crime was not directed at the assailants: see *infra*, para. 13-18.

13-13   See Glanville Williams, "The Theory of Excuses" [1982] Crim. L.R. 732.

13-18   Necessity was accepted as a defence to a charge of attempting to drive with an excess of alcohol in one's blood where the accused was trying to escape from three men who had already inflicted substantial injuries on him and were trying to smash the windows of his car which he had entered in an attempt to protect himself from further injury: *Tudhope* v. *Grubb*, 1983 S.C.C.R. 350 (Sh. Ct.).

13-20   For an example of the treatment of coercion as involving an over-powering of the will, see *Paquette* v. *The Queen* [1977] 2 S.C.R. 189, 197: "A person whose actions have been dictated by fears of death or of grievous bodily injury cannot be said to have formed a genuine intention to carry out an unlawful purpose with the person who has threatened him with those consequences if he fails to co-operate."

13-25   In *R.* v. *Fitzpatrick* [1977] N.I. 20 it was held that a member of an illegal organization cannot plead duress in respect of crimes committed against his will or in respect of his continued but unwilling association with the organization. "If a person behaves immorally by, for example, committing himself to an unlawful conspiracy, he ought not to be able to take advantage of the pressure exercised on him by his fellow criminals in order to put on when it suits him the breastplate of righteousness" at 31 D-E. The court also referred to the American rule that coercion is not available to someone who is culpably negligent or reckless in exposing himself to the risk of coercion.

13-26   It was held in *Thomson* v. *H.M. Advocate*, 1983 S.L.T. 682 that the defence of coercion can succeed only where the harm threatened is so imminent that it is not possible for the accused to seek the protection of the authorities. The extent of his participation in the crime and/or his restoration of the spoils or disclosure of the crime are not conditions for the application of the plea, but go only to credibility. The degree of coercion applied must be such that it would affect a reasonable person of normal resolution: *cf.* the law on provocation, *infra*, paras. 25-32 *et seq.*; *R.* v. *Graham (Paul)* [1982] 1 W.L.R. 294. The plea is not normally available to someone who joins what he knows to be a criminal gang: *cf. R.* v. *Fitzpatrick, supra*, para. 13-25. The law laid down in *Thomson* seems in line with that in other Commonwealth countries; *e.g. R.* v. *Teichelman* [1981] 2 N.Z.L.R. 64; *R.* v. *Dawson* [1978] V.R. 536; for a criticism of *Thomson*, see Alan Norrie, "The Defence of Coercion in Scots Criminal Law", 1984 S.L.T. (News) 13.

13-27   The availability of coercion as a defence to murder was conceded in the particular circumstances of *R.* v. *Graham (Paul)* [1982] 1 W.L.R. 294. The position of murder was reserved in *Thomson* v. *H.M. Advocate*, 1983 S.L.T. 682.

13-36   For a modern case on superior orders, see *Attorney-General's Reference (No. 1 of 1975)* [1977] A.C. 105.

CHAPTER 14

THEFT

14-15   It has been held in England that to take an article from a shelf in a supermarket, remove its price label and substitute one from a cheaper article, constitutes appropriation and is a completed theft, even though there is an intention to pay the lesser price: *R.* v. *Morris* [1983] 3 W.L.R. 697; *Oxford* v. *Peers* (1980) 72 Cr. App. R. 19. Such a case should, it is submitted, be treated in Scotland as an attempt to defraud the store of the goods or at least of the difference in price: compare *Kaur* v. *Chief Constable for Hampshire* [1981] 1 W.L.R. 578, which was disapproved in *R.* v. *Morris.*

It has also been held in England that where a person puts goods into the store's trolley intending not to pay for them, but changes his mind and abandons the trolley in the store there is no theft: *Eddy* v. *Niman* (1981) 73 Cr. App. R. 237.

14-21   The unusual case of *Mackenzie* v. *MacLean*, 1981 S.L.T. (Sh. Ct.) 40 perhaps owes more to a sense of proportion than to strict law.

14-24   The Burgh Police (Scotland) Act provisions are now replaced by ss. 67 to 75 of the Civic Government (Scotland) Act 1982.

Section 67(1) of that Act obliges any person taking possession of any property without the owner's authority in circumstances making it reasonable to infer that it has been lost or abandoned to take reasonable care of it and to deliver it, or report his finding of it, to a constable (or to its owner or possessor, or to the owner or occupier of any premises or land on which it was found, or to anyone apparently authorised to act on behalf of any of these persons) without unreasonable delay. Any person other than a constable, or the owner or possessor of the property to whom a finder makes a report under these provisions, is himself obliged to report the matter to a constable or to the owner or possessor: s. 67(4). Failure to do so without reasonable excuse is a summary offence: maximum penalty a fine of level 2: s. 67(6).

Any person who reports to a constable that he has taken possession of lost or abandoned property may be directed by the chief constable to deliver it to such person as the latter may direct, and failure to do so without reasonable excuse is an offence under the section punishable as above: s. 67(4); *quaere* whether "chief constable" here requires the personal intervention of that officer or of a specifically appointed deputy.

The chief constable is empowered to make arrangements for the custody of lost property, and is obliged to try to find the owner. After two months he may dispose of it if he thinks this appropriate in the circumstances, but he may do so earlier if it cannot be safely or conveniently kept, and he may return it to the owner at any time. If it is not claimed he can offer it to the finder or sell it. The chief constable may also order the owner to pay him such sum as he determines as a reward to the finder: ss. 68,70.

14-24   A disposal of property under these provisions to a person taking it in good faith vests ownership in that person subject to a right in the previous owner to recover possession within a year thereof: s. 71. This is the only way in which ownership of lost or abandoned property can be transferred: s. 73.

These provisions do not apply to property found on public transport premises or vehicles, or to dogs: s. 67(2).

14-33   For water see now Water (Scotland) Act 1980, Sched. 4, para. 31; maximum fine level 1.

14-34   Footnote 88. Maximum fine under s. 51 is level 2, and under s. 55 level 3: Criminal Justice Act 1982, Sched. 15.

14-42   Footnote 21. The reference should be to s. 536(2)(*c*); maximum fine now level 3: Merchant Shipping Act 1979, Sched. 6.

Footnote 22. Maximum fine now level 4: Merchant Shipping Act 1979, Sched. 6.

14-47   Footnote 65. See now Sale of Goods Act 1979, s. 18, r. 4.

14-50   A charge of embezzlement by a partner of funds received by him for the partnership was upheld by the High Court in *Peter Anthony Sumner*, Nov. 1983, unreported.

14-62   For a discussion of the position where a person who has complete control of a company is charged with theft from the company, see *Att.-Gen.'s Reference (No. 2 of 1982)* [1984] 2 W.L.R. 447.

Footnote 48. See now Sale of Goods Act 1979, ss. 24,25.

14-65   See Glanville Williams, "Temporary Appropriation should be Theft" [1981] Crim. L.R. 129.

14-65 to 14-76   It seems now to be accepted that temporary appropriation for a nefarious purpose is theft. In *Milne* v. *Tudhope*, 1981 J.C. 53 a builder who was doing work on a house on a fixed price contract refused to carry out remedial work without further payment, and removed parts of the house without the consent of the owner whom he told he would not return them unless he received more money. He was convicted of theft, on the view that "a clandestine taking, aimed at achieving a nefarious purpose, constitutes theft, even if the taker intends all along to return the thing when his purpose has been achieved." The conviction was upheld, the court saying that in certain exceptional cases an intention to deprive temporarily will suffice, and disapproving *Herron* v. *Best*. The exceptional circumstances in this case were that the accused was seeking to achieve an unlawful, even if not a criminal, purpose. The element of clandestinity is unimportant, since it means nothing more than that the owner was not aware of and had not authorised the removal, and indeed only the latter matters.

Milne v. *Tudhope* leaves us without any general principle for determining when temporary appropriation is enough. It might be argued that where the intention to return is conditional on the owner doing something which the accused is not entitled to require him to do,

**14-65
to
14-76**
there is a theft; or alternatively, and this may indeed be the same thing, it might be argued that there is theft where the circumstances also involve some other crime, such as extortion. But the court approved a general reference to taking for a nefarious purpose, which would mean, for example, that to borrow a key in order to commit housebreaking was clearly theft, and indeed that to borrow it to gain entry to premises in order there to engage in shamelessly indecent conduct was enough. *Milne* v. *Tudhope* may be another example of the tendency of Scots law to make broad "moral" pronouncements. It was followed by the trial judge in *Sandlan* v. *H.M. Advocate*, 1983 S.C.C.R. 71 where it was suggested that stock and books had been temporarily removed from a company's premises by its director in order to prevent auditors discovering shortages. Lord Stewart told the jury that where goods are removed clandestinely, that is to say, secretly, "such a taking . . ., aimed at achieving a nefarious purpose, constitutes theft even if the taker intends all along to return the things taken when his purpose has been achieved.": at 83.

See now also *Kidston* v. *Annan*, 1984 S.C.C.R. 20 in which *Milne* v. *Tudhope* was followed in the case of a person who was given property in order to make an estimate of the cost of repairing it and who refused to return the property unless he was paid for an uninstructed repair. In that case a reference to "holding goods to ransom" which had been made in *Milne* v. *Tudhope* was approved as describing a situation which constituted theft.

14-71
See also D.W. Elliott, "Dishonesty in Theft. A Dispensable Concept" [1982] Crim. L.R. 395. For the current state of English law, see Archbold (41st ed.) para. 17-32.

**14-77
to
14-79**
It was held in *Kivlin* v. *Milne*, 1979 S.L.T. (Notes) 2 that where a car was unlawfully taken and left in a place where the owner was not liable to discover it by his own investigations the sheriff was entitled to infer an intention permanently to deprive. It was accepted, however, that it would always be a question of circumstances in each case whether that intention had been established. On the other hand, *McLeod* v. *Mason and Ors.*, 1981 S.C.C.R. 75 indicates that in the absence of evidence that the accused intended only to contravene section 175 of the Road Traffic Act an intention to steal is to be presumed: see the commentary at 1981 S.C.C.R. 78.

14-79
Footnote 31. *Lambie* v. *H.M.A.* is now reported at 1973 J.C. 53.

14-85
Footnote 45. See also *supra*, paras. 14-65 to 14-76.

Chapter 15

AGGRAVATED THEFTS AND ALLIED OFFENCES

15-22
The relevant value is now level 4: Criminal Justice Act 1982, Sched. 7.

15-29
Footnote 9. See now the 2nd edition of Walker on *Delict* (Edinburgh, 1981).

15-34 The *McKnight* v. *Davies* approach was preferred in *Barclay* v. *Douglas*, 1983 S.C.C.R. 224 where A was given the keys of B's car so that he might drive a short distance to B's house. On his way to the car A met his girl friend and took her for a run in the car in the course of which he was stopped by the police. He was convicted of a contravention of section 175.

Where consent is obtained by fraud and the use of the vehicle is within the terms of that consent, there is no contravention of section 175: *Whittaker* v. *Campbell* [1983] 3 W.L.R. 676.

15-41 Footnote 39. Section 34 of the Mental Health (Scotland) Act 1960 is repealed by the Mental Health (Amendment) (Scotland) Act 1983.

15-49 Maximum fine now level 1: Criminal Justice Act 1982, Sched. 15.

15-51 Section 4 of the Vagrancy Act 1824 is repealed by the Civic Government (Scotland) Act 1982.

15-52 Footnote 63. Maximum fine now level 3: Merchant Shipping Act 1979, Sched. 6.

Footnote 64. Maximum fine now level 2: Merchant Shipping Act 1979, Sched. 6.

15-54 Section 21(4A) of the Copyright Act 1956, as inserted by s. 1 of the Copyright Act 1956 (Amendment) Act 1982 provides:

> "Any person who, at a time when copyright subsists in a sound recording or in a cinematograph film, by way of trade has in his possession any article which he knows to be an infringing copy of the sound recording or cinematograph film, as the case may be, shall be guilty of an offence under this subsection."

Offences relating to sound recordings or films under subss. (1)(*b*) or (*c*) or (4A) are punishable by two months' imprisonment and a fine of level 5 and under subss. (1)(*a*) or (*d*) or (2) by a fine and two years' imprisonment on indictment, and a fine on summary conviction. Other offences are punishable as follows: subss. (1) or (2), a fine of level 1 per article up to a maximum of level 3 for any transaction and two months' imprisonment; and subss. (3) or (5), a fine of level 3 and such imprisonment: see Copyright (Amendment) Act 1983.

15-61 In a charge of opening a lockfast car with intent to steal it is not necessary to specify or prove whether the intention was to steal the car or its contents: *McLeod* v. *Mason and Ors.*, 1981 S.C.C.R. 75, a case which appears to achieve much the same result as section 9 of the English Criminal Attempts Act 1981.

15-62 to 15-71 Sections 7 and 20 of the Prevention of Crimes Act 1871, s. 4 of the Vagrancy Act 1824 and s. 409 of the Burgh Police (Scotland) Act 1892 are repealed by the Civic Government (Scotland) Act 1982.

Section 57(1) of the Civic Government (Scotland) Act 1982 provides:

> "Any person who, without lawful authority to be there, is found in or on a building or other premises, whether enclosed or not, or in its curtilage or in a vehicle or vessel so that, in all the circumstances, it may reasonably be

inferred that he intended to commit theft there shall be guilty of an offence and liable, on summary conviction, to a fine not exceeding [level 4] or to imprisonment for a period not exceeding 3 months or to both."

"Theft" includes any aggravation of theft including robbery: *ibid.*, s. 57(2).

Section 58(1) of the Civic Government (Scotland) Act 1982 provides:

> "Any person who, being a person to whom this section applies—
>> (*a*) has or has recently had in his possession any tool or other object from the possession of which it may reasonably be inferred that he intended to commit theft or has committed theft; and
>> (*b*) is unable to demonstrate satisfactorily that his possession of such tool or other object is or was not for the purposes of committing theft
>
> shall be guilty of an offence and liable, on summary conviction, to a fine not exceeding [level 4] or to imprisonment for a period not exceeding 3 months or to both."

The section applies to persons with two or more convictions for theft which are not spent in terms of the Rehabilitation of Offenders Act 1974: s. 58(4). "Theft" includes any aggravation of theft, including robbery: s. 58(5).

"Recent possession" in this context means possession within 14 days of the accused's arrest for contravention of s. 58(1) or of the issue of a warrant for his arrest therefor, or of any earlier date at which he is first served with a complaint therefor: s. 58(2).

It will be noted that these provisions are much narrower than the older ones. In particular, they are limited to theft and robbery, and do not extend even to other crimes of dishonesty.

CHAPTER 16

ROBBERY

16-19 The Hijacking Act 1971 is repealed by the Aviation Security Act 1982. Section 1 is replaced by s. 1 of the latter Act, which provides:

> "(1) A person on board an aircraft in flight who unlawfully, by the use of force or by threats of any kind, seizes the aircraft or exercises control of it commits the offence of hijacking, whatever his nationality, whatever the State in which the aircraft is registered and whether the aircraft is in the United Kingdom or elsewhere, but subject to subsection (2) below.
> (2) If—
>> (*a*) the aircraft is used in military, customs or police service, or
>> (*b*) both the place of take-off and the place of landing are in the territory of the State in which the aircraft is registered,
> subsection (1) above shall not apply unless—
>>> (i) the person seizing or exercising control of the aircraft is a United Kingdom national; or
>>> (ii) his act is committed in the United Kingdom; or
>>> (iii) the aircraft is registered in the United Kingdom or is used in the military or customs service of the United Kingdom or in

the service of any police force in the United Kingdom.

(3) A person who commits the offence of hijacking shall be liable, on conviction on indictment, to imprisonment for life.

(4) If the Secretary of State by order made by statutory instrument declares—

(a) that any two or more States named in the order have established an organisation or agency which operates aircraft; and

(b) that one of those States has been designated as exercising, for aircraft so operated, the powers of the State of registration,

the State declared under paragraph (b) of this subsection shall be deemed for the purposes of this section to be the State in which any aircraft so operated is registered; but in relation to such an aircraft subsection (2)(b) above shall have effect as if it referred to the territory of any one of the States named in the order.

(5) For the purposes of this section the territorial waters of any State shall be treated as part of its territory."

A United Kingdom national is someone who is
(a) a British citizen, a British Dependent Territories citizen or a British overseas citizen; or
(b) a person who under the British Nationality Act 1981 is a British subject; or
(c) a British protected person (within the meaning of that Act): Aviation Security Act 1982, s. 38(1).

CHAPTER 17

EMBEZZLEMENT

17-28   A partner may be convicted of embezzlement from his firm: *Peter Anthony Sumner*, High Court on appeal, November 1983, unreported.

CHAPTER 18

COMMON LAW FRAUD

18-06   The applicability of *R.* v. *Charles* [1977] A.C. 177 to credit cards was affirmed by the House of Lords in *R.* v. *Lambie* [1982] A.C. 449. Presentation of a cheque card or credit card constitutes a representation of actual authority from the bank or the card company to use the card for the transaction in question. It is for the jury to decide whether it was that representation which induced the dupe to hand over the goods, and it is to be expected that in practice they will decide that it was.

18-54   See also *Macdonald* v. *Tudhope*, 1983 S.C.C.R. 341.

CHAPTER 19

STATUTORY FRAUDS

19-05   Section 187 is extended by Sched. 3 to the Companies Act 1981 to include acting as liquidator and being concerned in the promotion or formation of a company.

19-09   Maximum penalty seven years' imprisonment and a fine on indictment, six months and a fine on summary conviction: Companies Act 1980, Sched. 2.

19-10   Maximum penalty as for a contravention of s. 328, *supra.*

19-11   Maximum penalty now two years' imprisonment and a fine on indictment, six months and a fine on summary conviction: Companies Act 1980, Sched. 2.

Add new paragraph **19-11a**:

19-11a   *Fraudulent trading.* Section 332(3) of the Companies Act 1948, as amended by Sched. 2 to the Companies Act 1980, provides:

> "Where any business of a company is carried on [with intent to defraud creditors of the company or creditors of any other person or for any fraudulent purpose], every person who was knowingly a party to the carrying on of the business in manner aforesaid, shall be liable on conviction on indictment to [seven years' imprisonment and a fine, and on summary conviction to six months' imprisonment and a fine.]"

The former rule that offences under section 332(3) could be committed only during a winding up — *R. v. Schildkamp* [1971] A.C. 1 — is altered by s. 96 of the Companies Act 1981 which provides that s. 332(3) shall apply "whether or not the company has been or is in the course of being wound up."

It has been held that the collection and distribution of assets constitutes "carrying on business", which is not the same as carrying on trade: *Re Sarflax Ltd.* [1979] Ch. 592. The same case held that merely to prefer one creditor to another was not fraudulent.

19-12   Section 438 of and Sched. 15 to the Companies Act 1948 are repealed by the Companies Act 1980.

19-13   Maximum penalty under s. 44 two years' imprisonment and a fine on indictment, six months and a fine on summary conviction: Companies Act 1980, Sched. 2.

Section 438 is now repealed: *supra*, para. 19-12.

Footnote 39. Maximum penalty under s. 421 is a fine on indictment: Companies Act 1980, Sched. 2.

19-14   Maximum penalty a fine on indictment: Companies Act 1980, Sched. 2.

19-15   Maximum penalty with effect from 1st May 1984, £400 on summary conviction, and £40 a day for any continuing contravention after conviction: Companies Act 1980, Sched. 2; Increase of Criminal Penalties etc. (Scotland) Order 1984.

19-16   Maximum penalty seven years' imprisonment and a fine on indictment, six months' and a fine on summary conviction: Companies Act 1980, Sched. 2.

19-17   See also s. 149 of the Companies Act 1948, as inserted by s. 1 of the Companies Act 1981. Maximum penalty now a fine of the prescribed sum and one-tenth of that sum a day for any contravention following on conviction: Companies Act 1980, Sched. 2.

19-18   The Protection of Depositors Act 1963 is repealed by the Banking Act 1979.

19-19   The authority for the amendments originally made by the Protection of Depositors Act 1963 is now the Banking Act 1979, Sched. 6.

19-20   Section 63 of the Insurance Companies Act 1974 is repealed by the Insurance Companies Act 1982, and is re-enacted in s. 73 of that Act: maximum penalty two years' imprisonment and a fine on indictment; a fine on summary conviction: s. 81. See also s. 14, which deals with false statements to obtain authorisation.

19-21   This offence requires dishonesty for its commission: *R.* v. *Cox and Hodges* (1982) 75 Cr. App. R. 291.

19-23   The Protection of Depositors Act 1963 is repealed by the Banking Act 1979, s. 1 of which prohibits the taking of deposits in the course of business except by banks or other specified or licensed institutions: maximum penalty two years' imprisonment and a fine on indictment; a fine on summary conviction. Advertisement is controlled by the Bank of England, and by regulations; breaches of regulations or of directions issued by the Bank are offences punishable as above: ss. 34,35.

19-24   Section 1 of the Protection of Depositors Act 1963 is replaced by s. 39 of the Banking Act 1979, with some alterations in the meaning of "deposit": see s. 39(2).

19-26   It has been held that the fact that a car is used for his business by a self-employed owner does not make his sale of it a sale in the course of trade or business: *Davies* v. *Sumner* [1984] 1 W.L.R. 405. But see Ian Lloyd, "Consumer Protection. Sales 'in the course of a business'" (1984) 29 J.L.S. 147; *Buchanan-Jardine* v. *Hamilink and Anr.*, 1981 S.L.T. (Notes) 60.

19-42   It has been said that a defence of due diligence cannot succeed unless the precaution of making a disclaimer has been taken: *Simmons* v. *Potter* [1975] R.T.R. 347; *Crook* v. *Howells Garages (Newport) Ltd.* [1980] R.T.R. 434. On the other hand, it has been pointed out that a disclaimer is not a defence in terms of s. 24, but evidence that no

19-42 representation was made: *Wandsworth LBC* v. *Bentley* [1980] R.T.R. 429. It has also been suggested that to wind down an odometer to nought might be a way of avoiding making any representation as to mileage, since no one would be misled by it into believing it to be a true record: *Lill Holdings* v. *White* [1979] R.T.R. 120.

> Footnote 20. Add: *Wandsworth LBC* v. *Bentley* [1980] R.T.R. 429.

19-44 It has been said that the act or default must be an unlawful one: *Lill Holdings* v. *White* [1979] R.T.R. 120, Wien, J. at 125.

19-46 Sections 162 and 164 of the Customs and Excise Act 1952 are repealed by the Alcoholic Liquor Duties Act 1979 and re-enacted by ss. 71 and 73 respectively of the latter Act: maximum penalty a fine of level 3, and forfeiture. Section 45 of the Act of 1952 is now s. 50 of the Customs and Excise Management Act 1979.

19-48 Section 91 of the Patents Act 1949 is repealed by the Patents Act 1977. Section 91(1) is replaced by s. 110 of that Act which provides, inter alia:

> "(1) If a person falsely represents that anything disposed of by him for value is a patented product he shall, subject to the following provisions of this section, be liable on summary conviction to a fine [of level 4]."

Subsection (2) provides that where the article has on it "patent" or any other expression implying that it is patented, anyone who disposes of it for value is taken to represent that it is a patented product. Subsection (3) provides that s. 110(1) shall not apply where the patent is revoked and a sufficient period has not elapsed to enable the accused to take steps to ensure that the representation is not made. Subsection (4) provides a general defence of due diligence.

Section 91(2) is replaced by s. 112 of the 1977 Act: maximum fine now level 5.

It is also an offence falsely to represent that a patent has been applied for in respect of an article disposed of for value where no application has been made, or where any application made has been withdrawn or refused. There is a defence of due diligence: Patents Act 1977, s. 111; maximum penalty a fine of level 4.

19-52 See now Sale of Goods Act 1979.

19-53 Footnote 44. See *Skinner* v. *MacLean*, 1979 S.L.T. (Notes) 35 which treats *Frew* v. *Gunning* as very special, and makes it clear that the facts that a sale is made in error and the error later brought to the notice of the buyer do not affect the seller's responsibility.

19-55 *Morton* v. *Green* was followed in the recent case of *Goldup* v. *Manson Ltd.* [1982] Q.B. 161 where it was held that the court is not obliged to accept uncontradicted expert evidence as to what the standard should be in relation to the fat content of beef. It is for the prosecution to show that the customer was demanding mince containing significantly less fat than was supplied.

19-61   Footnote 64. Maximum fine now level 3: Weights and Measures Act 1979, s. 18.

19-63   See also Weights and Measures Act 1979.
Footnote 83. See now Units of Measurement Regulations 1980.

19-64   Maximum fine now level 5: Weights and Measures Act 1979, s. 18.

19-65   The offence of possession under this section is one of strict responsibility, but can be committed only by a person who has actual control of the weights; the mere fact that a licensee is the only person who can lawfully use liquor measures in a sale does not make him their possessor: *Bellerby* v. *Carle* [1983] 2 A.C. 101, although if short measure is actually sold he is liable as the seller: *MacDonald* v. *Smith*, 1979 J.C. 55. Maximum penalty for an offence under s. 16(3) is six months' imprisonment and a fine of level 5: Weights and Measures Act 1979, s. 18; maximum penalty under s. 16(1) is a fine of level 5.

19-66   On the vexed question of the "head" of a glass of beer, see *Dean* v. *Scottish and Newcastle Breweries*, 1977 J.C. 90.

Footnote 72. Maximum penalty now a fine of level 5: Weights and Measures Act 1979, s. 18.

19-70   A licensee is responsible for a sale by a barman even if they are fellow employees: *MacDonald* v. *Smith*, 1979 J.C. 55.

19-85 to 19-91   The Coinage Offences Act 1936, the Bank Notes Forgery Act 1801 and the Bank Notes (Forgery) Act 1805 are repealed by the Forgery and Counterfeiting Act 1981 which creates the following offences. (The Act followed on the Law Commission's Report on Forgery and Counterfeit Currency, 1973 (Law Com. No. 55)).

COUNTERFEITING. Section 14:

"(1) It is an offence for a person to make a counterfeit of a currency note or of a protected coin, intending that he or another shall pass or tender it as genuine.
(2) It is an offence for a person to make a counterfeit of a currency note or of a protected coin without lawful authority or excuse."

Maximum penalty under subs. (1) is ten years' imprisonment and a fine on indictment, and under subs. (2) two years' imprisonment and a fine on indictment. The maximum imprisonment on summary conviction is six months in each case: s. 22.

PASSING COUNTERFEIT NOTES OR COINS. Section 15:

"(1) It is an offence for a person—
    (*a*) to pass or tender as genuine any thing which is, and which he knows or believes to be, a counterfeit of a currency note or of a protected coin; or
    (*b*) to deliver to another any thing which is, and which he knows or believes to be, such a counterfeit, intending that the person to whom it is delivered or another shall pass or tender it as genuine.
(2) It is an offence for a person to deliver to another, without lawful authority or excuse, any thing which is, and which he knows or believes to be, a counterfeit of a currency note or of a protected coin."

Maximum penalty as for s. 14(1) and (2) respectively.

Possession of counterfeit notes and coins. Section 16:

"(1) It is an offence for a person to have in his custody or under his control any thing which is, and which he knows or believes to be, a counterfeit of a currency note or of a protected coin, intending either to pass or tender it as genuine or to deliver it to another with the intention that he or another shall pass or tender it as genuine.

(2) It is an offence for a person to have in his custody or under his control, without lawful authority or excuse, any thing which is, and which he knows or believes to be, a counterfeit of a currency note or of a protected coin.

(3) It is immaterial for the purposes of subsections (1) and (2) above that a coin or note is not in a fit state to be passed or tendered or that the making or counterfeiting of a coin or note has not been finished or perfected."

Maximum penalties as for s. 14(1) and (2) respectively.

Possession of implements. It is an offence to make or have in one's custody or control anything intended for use by oneself or others to make a counterfeit note or coin intended to be passed as genuine: s. 17(1); maximum penalty as for s. 14(1).

It is also an offence to make or have in one's custody or control, without lawful authority or excuse, anything one knows to be designed or adapted for making a counterfeit currency note: s. 17(2); maximum penalty as for s. 14(2). It is also an offence to make or have in one's custody or control anything one knows to be capable of imparting to anything a resemblance to all or part of either side of a protected coin or of the reverse of the image on either side of a protected coin: s. 17(3); maximum penalty as for s. 14(2). It is a defence to this last offence to prove that one acted with Treasury permission or with other lawful authority or excuse: s. 17(4).

Reproduction of imitations. It is an offence to reproduce any British currency note or any part of such a note on any substance or scale without written permission from the relevant authority: s. 18. It is also an offence to make, sell or distribute, or have custody or control of, an imitation British coin in connection with a scheme intended to promote the sale of any product or the making of contracts for the supply of any service, without prior Treasury consent in writing to such sale or distribution: s. 19; maximum penalty under these sections is a fine on indictment.

Definitions. "Currency note" is defined by s. 27(1) as follows:

(a) any note which—
　(i) has been lawfully issued in England and Wales, Scotland, Northern Ireland, any of the Channel Islands, the Isle of Man or the Republic of Ireland; and
　(ii) is or has been customarily used as money in the country where it was issued; and
　(iii) is payable on demand; or
(b) any note which—
　(i) has been lawfully issued in some country other than those

19-85
to
19-91

mentioned in paragraph (*a*)(i) above; and
    (ii) is customarily used as money in that country."

A British currency note, in terms of s. 18 is a currency note issued in England and Wales, Scotland or Northern Ireland.

"Protected coin" is any coin customarily used as money in any country, or specified in the Forgery and Counterfeiting (Protected Coin) Order 1981, s. 27(1).

"British coin" in s. 19 is any coin which is legal tender in the United Kingdom (see Coinage Act 1971, s. 2), and imitation British coin is anything resembling a British coin in shape, size and substance.

"Counterfeiting" is defined by s. 28 as follows:

> "(1) For the purposes of this Part of this Act a thing is a counterfeit of a currency note or of a protected coin—
>   (*a*) if it is not a currency note or a protected coin but resembles a currency note or protected coin (whether on one side only or on both) to such an extent that it is reasonably capable of passing for a currency note or protected coin of that description; or
>   (*b*) if it is a currency note or protected coin which has been so altered that it is reasonably capable of passing for a currency note or protected coin of some other description.
>   (2) For the purposes of this Part of this Act—
>   (*a*) a thing consisting of one side only of a currency note, with or without the addition of other material, is a counterfeit of such a note;
>   (*b*) a thing consisting—
>   (i) of parts of two or more currency notes; or
>   (ii) of parts of a currency note, or of parts of two or more currency notes, with the addition of other material,
>   is capable of being a counterfeit of a currency note.
>   (3) References in this Part of this Act to passing or tendering a counterfeit of a currency note or a protected coin are not to be construed as confined to passing or tendering it as legal tender."

19-99   Footnote 36. The Bank Notes (Forgery) (Scotland) Act 1820 and s. 380(15) of the Burgh Police (Scotland) Act 1892 are repealed by the Forgery and Counterfeiting Act 1981.

19-101   The Counterfeit Currency (Convention) Act 1935 is repealed by the Forgery and Counterfeiting Act 1981.

19-102   National Insurance and Industrial Injuries Insurance are now abolished.

19-108   "Fraudulently" means with intent to deceive, and does not require an intent to defraud: *R.* v. *Clayton* (1980) 72 Cr. App. R. 135.

19-117   These provisions are repealed by the Civic Government (Scotland) Act 1982.

19-119   This provision disappeared with the repeal of s. 4 of the Vagrancy Act 1824 by the Civic Government (Scotland) Act 1982.

19-123   Maximum penalty a fine of level 4 or three months' imprisonment: Criminal Justice Act 1982, Sched. 6.

19-125   The Medical Act 1956 is repealed by the Medical Act 1983, and s. 31 is re-enacted in s. 49 of the latter Act: maximum penalties a fine of level 5, which is to be paid to the treasurer of the General Medical Council.

19-130   Section 12 of the Nurses (Scotland) Act 1951 and s. 9 of the Midwives (Scotland) Act 1951 are repealed by the Nurses, Midwives and Health Visitors Act 1979, s. 14 of which penalises the making and the causing or permitting others to make false representations as to one's qualifications or registered status, as well as making such representations about other people, all with intent to deceive: maximum penalty a fine of level 4.

19-131   The Solicitors (Scotland) Act 1933 is repealed by the Solicitors (Scotland) Act 1980, and s. 36 is re-enacted in s. 31 of the latter Act: maximum penalty a fine of level 3 and one month's imprisonment: s. 63(1); 1975 Act, s. 289F(3), (8).

19-135   The subsection quoted is subs. (3) of s. 146: maximum penalty now a fine of level 5 and three months' imprisonment: Social Security Act 1981, Sched. 1.

It was held in *Barrass* v. *Reeve* [1981] 1 W.L.R. 408 that it is an offence under this section to make any statement known to be untrue, even if the statement is not made with intent to obtain benefit to which one is not entitled, but only in order to deceive an employer. The false statement in that case was made on a sickness benefit claim form and related to the date on which the accused became unfit for work, he having in fact worked for someone else for two days after that date, and being unwilling to admit this lest he lose his job. The accused was not aware that he was entitled to benefit for these two days. Waller, L.J. said, ". . . the plain words of this subsection are covered if a person, for the purpose of obtaining any benefit or other payments under this Act, knowingly makes any false statement . . . There are no words to say 'with intent to obtain money' or anything of that sort": at 413C-D.

In *Clear* v. *Smith* [1981] 1 W.L.R. 399 the accused was charged with falsely declaring that he had not worked when in fact he had delivered scrap metal to dealers on behalf of others without payment, although he sometimes received petrol for the journeys he made. It was held that "work" was not limited to paid work, and that provided a statement was made dishonestly it was not necessary to show an intention to defraud. The justices had held that the accused knew that he was doing work dealing in scrap so that no defence of error was available, even assuming that an error as to the meaning of "work" was one of fact. Lord Widgery, C.J. said that the question was one of fact and degree, and went on, "One cannot possibly lay down as a general proposition that an unpaid activity is not work. As was suggested in argument, no housewife would be ready to accept that proposition with equanimity. On the other hand, it does not follow that every activity which is backed up by remuneration is work": at 406A-B.

19-136   Section 21 of the Supplementary Benefits Act 1976, as substituted

19-136 by s. 14(5) of the Social Security (Miscellaneous Provisions) Act 1977, provides as follows:

> "If any person, for the purpose of obtaining supplementary benefit or any other payment under this Act for himself or another person or for any other purpose connected with this Act—
>
> (*a*) makes any statement or representation which he knows to be false, or
>
> (*b*) produces or furnishes, or causes or knowingly allows to be produced or furnished, any document or information which he knows to be false in a material particular,
>
> he shall be liable on summary conviction to a fine [of level 5 on the standard scale] or to imprisonment for a term not exceeding three months or to both": see Social Security Act 1981, Sched. 1.

19-137 The Family Allowances Act 1965 is repealed by the Child Benefit Act 1975, s. 11(1) of which creates an offence in relation to child benefit in the same terms as those of s. 21 of the Supplementary Benefits Act 1976, *supra*, para. 19-136.

19-138 Footnote 1. The reference to the Gas Act 1972 should be to Sched. 4, para. 20. For water see now Water (Scotland) Act 1980, Sched. 4, para. 32. For electricity see Criminal Justice Act 1982, Sched. 15; maximum penalty a fine of level 3.

Add new paragraph **19-138a**:

19-138a *Telephones.* Dishonest use of a public telecommunication system with intent to avoid payment is an offence under section 48 of the British Telecommunications Act 1981: maximum penalty two years' imprisonment and a fine on indictment, six months and a fine on summary conviction.

19-139 The Protection of Aircraft Act 1973 is repealed by the Aviation Security Act 1982. Section 2(3) and (4) are re-enacted by s. 3(3) and (4) of the latter Act. The offence of making false statements in response to a requirement made by the Secretary of State of aircraft operators or aerodrome managers is now contained in s. 11(5)(*b*) of the Act of 1982.

19-142 Footnote 7. Section 16(7) of the Dentists Act 1957 is repealed by s. 13(2) of the Dentists Act 1983. The Nurses (Scotland) Act 1951 and the Midwives (Scotland) Act 1951 are repealed by the Nurses, Midwives and Health Visitors Act 1979; for the offence of falsely claiming to possess a relevant professional qualification, see s. 14: maximum penalty a fine of level 4.

CHAPTER 20

RESET

20-02 Footnote 6. See also *McRae* v. *H.M.A.*, 1975 J.C. 34.

20-05 A husband is not entitled to the benefit of this rule which is limited to a wife, and even in her case to the concealment of property in order to protect her husband from detection or punishment: *Smith* v. *Watson*,

20-05 1982 S.C.C.R. 15. It does not apply to a wife who uses the property, or to her continued concealment of it after her husband has been sentenced, so that *Clark* v. *Mone* is of little value as an authority.

20-10 Footnote 42. Section 439 of the Burgh Police (Scotland) Act 1892 and s. 13 of the Prevention of Crimes Act 1871 are repealed by the Civic Government (Scotland) Act 1982.

20-15 Footnote 54. Insert at the beginning of the note: *Backhurst* v. *MacNaughton*, 1981 S.C.C.R. 6.

20-17 Where, however, the passenger remains silent and does not attempt to run away when the vehicle is stopped by the police, there may be insufficient evidence to convict him of reset: *Hipson* v. *Tudhope*, 1983 S.C.C.R. 247.

20-21 Section 7 of the Public Stores Act 1875 is repealed by the Criminal Law Act 1977, Sched. 12.

Add new paragraph **20-21a**:

20-21a *Value Added Tax.* Section 39(4) of the Value Added Tax Act 1983 makes it an offence to acquire possession of or deal with any goods having reason to believe that tax on the supply or importation of the goods has been or will be evaded: maximum penalty a fine of level 5 or three times the amount of tax whichever is greater.

20-22 Section 13 of the Prevention of Crimes Act 1871 will be repealed by the Civic Government (Scotland) Act 1982 and metal dealing will be controlled by ss. 28 to 37 of the latter Act.

20-23
20-24 These provisions are repealed by the Forgery and Counterfeiting Act 1981.

20-25 Section 409 of the Burgh Police (Scotland) Act 1892 is repealed by the Civic Government (Scotland) Act 1982, and replaced by s. 58 of the latter Act which is in the following terms:

"(1) Any person who, being a person to whom this section applies—
(*a*) has or has recently had in his possession any tool or other object from the possession of which it may reasonably be inferred that he intended to commit theft or has committed theft; and
(*b*) is unable to demonstrate satisfactorily that his possession of such tool or other object is or was not for the purposes of committing theft
shall be guilty of an offence and liable, on summary conviction, to a fine not exceeding [level 4] or to imprisonment for a period not exceeding 3 months or to both.
(2) For the purposes of subsection (1) above, a person shall have recently had possession of a tool or other object if he had possession of it within 14 days before the date of—
(*a*) his arrest without warrant for the offence of having so possessed it in contravention of subsection (1) above; or
(*b*) the issue of a warrant for his arrest for that offence; or
(*c*) if earlier, the service upon him of the first complaint alleging that he has committed that offence.

(3) Where a court convicts a person of an offence under this section or discharges him absolutely or makes a probation order in relation to him in respect of such an offence it may order the forfeiture of any tool or other object in respect of the possession of which he was convicted or discharged absolutely, or, as the case may be, the probation order was made.

(4) This section applies to a person who has two or more convictions for theft which are not, for the purposes of the Rehabilitation of Offenders Act 1974, spent convictions.

(5) In this section 'theft' includes any aggravation of theft including robbery."

Section 438 will also be repealed by the Civic Government (Scotland) Act 1982.

Section 26 of the latter Act will make it an offence for anyone to give a false name or address when selling anything to a second-hand dealer: maximum penalty a fine of level 3.

CHAPTER 21

EXTORTION AND CORRUPTION

21-10   See also *Rae* v. *Donnelly*, 1982 S.C.C.R. 148: threat to expose sexual relationship if victim did not drop action for wrongful dismissal.

21-20   It has been held in England that it is necessary for the Crown to prove a specific intent to harass a person believed to be a residential occupier, and that no offence is committed where the accused believes on reasonable grounds that the person harassed is a squatter: *R.* v. *Phekoo* [1981] 1 W.L.R. 1117; but *cf. R.* v. *Kimber* [1983] 1 W.L.R. 1118.

21-26   No offence is committed under this paragraph where the document is an internal one passing only between an employee and his employers: *R.* v. *Tweedie* [1984] 2 W.L.R. 608.

21-27   Maximum penalty a fine of level 2 in each case: Merchant Shipping Act 1979, Sched. 6.

CHAPTER 22

DAMAGE TO PROPERTY

22-01   Malicious mischief may be committed by causing economic loss even where there is no damage to any corporeal property, at least where the loss is caused by doing something to such property as, for example, by turning a switch on or off and so activating or preventing the activation of machinery or power: *H.M.A.* v. *Wilson*, 1984 S.L.T. 117. It may

22-01 also be caused by deflating a tyre: *Peter Penman*, High Court on appeal, March 1984, unreported.

22-13 Insert new paragraph **22-13a**:

22-13a *Vandalism.* Section 78(1) and (2) of the Criminal Justice (Scotland) Act 1980 provides:

> "(1) Subject to subsection (2) below, any person who, without reasonable excuse, wilfully or recklessly destroys or damages any property belonging to another shall be guilty of the offence of vandalism.
> (2) It shall not be competent to charge acts which constitute the offence of wilful fire-raising as vandalism under this section."

Maximum penalty in the district court 60 days' imprisonment and a fine of level 3, in the sheriff court three (or in the case of a subsequent offence six) months' imprisonment and a fine of level 5: see 1975 Act, s. 289E(4)(*b*), as inserted by Criminal Justice Act 1982, s. 54.

This provision appears to have been designed to single out those kinds of malicious mischief commonly referred to as vandalism, but it is frequently used for any kind of malicious mischief, even on indictment (as an additional charge where s. 457A(4) of the 1975 Act, as inserted by s. 55(1) of the Criminal Justice Act 1982, applies) where the only effect of libelling the statutory charge is to limit the court's powers of punishment.

22-15 On the Telegraph Act 1878, see *Post Office* v. *Hampshire C.C.* [1980] Q.B. 124.

References to telephone kiosks or cabinets are removed from the Post Office Act 1953 by the British Telecommunications Act 1981.

Footnote 37. Penalty now payable to British Telecommunications.

22-16 The Protection of Aircraft Act 1973 is repealed and re-enacted by the Aviation Security Act 1982.

22-17 The principal provision dealing with interference with water supplies is now the Water (Scotland) Act 1980, Sched. 4, para. 33. Section 380(14) of the Burgh Police (Scotland) Act 1892 will be repealed by the Civic Government (Scotland) Act 1982. Injury to electric lines, meters or fittings is dealt with in the South of Scotland Electricity Order Confirmation Act 1956 and the North of Scotland Electricity Order Confirmation Act 1958; maximum penalty a fine of level 3; Criminal Justice Act 1982, Sched. 15, paras. 9 to 12. Injury to water meters etc. is now dealt with under the Water (Scotland) Act 1980, Sched. 4, para. 32.

22-18 "Explosive" is defined in s. 3 of the Explosives Act 1875 as including substances "used or manufactured with a view to produce a practical effect by explosion or a pyrotechnic effect", and includes petrol bombs: *R.* v. *Bouch* [1983] Q.B. 246.

22-19 "Explosive" has the same meaning in the Explosive Substances Act 1883 as in the Explosives Act 1875: *R.* v. *Wheatley* [1979] 1 W.L.R.

22-19 144, and includes a petrol bomb made in a milk bottle whose main effect is to produce a fireball: *R.* v. *Bouch* [1983] Q.B. 246. Although the ingredients of a mixture of air and petrol in a milk bottle may not in themselves be in such proportions as to be an explosive substance the fact that the bottle will become a fireball when it is broken makes the petrol, bottle and accompanying wick, materials for making an explosive substance as defined in s. 9.

22-20 "Lawful object" may in some exceptional cases include the defence of person or property from imminent attack: *Att-Gen's Reference (No. 2 of 1983)* [1984] 2 W.L.R. 465.

Footnote 49. *Black* v. *H.M.A.* is now reported at 1974 J.C. 43.

CHAPTER 23

MURDER

23-01 See also D.J. Lanham, "Murder by Instigating Suicide" [1980] Crim. L.R. 215.

23-08 Footnote 29. Add: Walking into the path of a car so as to cause the driver to take action to avoid a collision, and then hitting the car, shouting, swearing, opening the driver's door, struggling with him, trying to let one of the tyres down, and placing the driver who had a weak heart in such a state of fear, alarm and exhaustion that he died there and then: *John Mason Taylor*, Criminal Appeal Court, June 1975, unreported; pushing someone who falls against another person who falls and sustains an injury from which he dies: *R.* v. *Mitchell* [1983] Q.B. 741; injecting a dangerous drug: *Finlayson* v. *H.M.A.*, 1979 J.C. 33. There is a form of manslaughter in English law known as "manslaughter by flight" which occurs when the victim dies as a result of, *e.g.* tripping while running away from an attack from which he fears imminent injury, the fear being caused by the conduct of the accused: *D.P.P.* v. *Daley* [1980] A.C. 237.

23-18 Footnote 78. *Brennan* v. *H.M.A.* is now reported at 1977 J.C. 38.

23-26 Footnote 16. See also *Robt. Paul Dunn*, Criminal Appeal Court, Jan. 1980, unreported. *D.P.P.* v. *Stonehouse* is now reported at [1978] A.C. 55.

23-29 Footnote 33a. *Brennan* v. *H.M.A.* is now reported at 1977 J.C. 38.

CHAPTER 25

VOLUNTARY CULPABLE HOMICIDE

25-01   Footnote 3. ⎫
25-08   Footnote 17. ⎬   *Brennan* v. *H.M.A.* is now reported at 1977 J.C. 38.
 ⎭

25-09   See M. Wasik, "Partial Excuses in Criminal Law" (1982) 45 M.L.R. 516.

25-29   Verbal provocation was left to the jury in *Stobbs* v. *H.M.A.*, 1983 S.C.C.R. 190.

25-33   Footnote 4a. *Brennan* v. *H.M.A.* is now reported at 1977 J.C. 38.

25-38   In *R.* v. *Camplin* [1978] A.C. 705 (see Celia Wells, "The Death Penalty for Provocation" [1978] Crim. L.R. 662), where the accused was a fifteen-year-old boy, the House of Lords preferred *McGregor* to *Bedder* v. *D.P.P.* [1954] 1 W.L.R. 1119. Lord Diplock said, "But to require old heads upon young shoulders is inconsistent with the law's compassion to human infirmity to which Sir Michael Foster [*Crown Cases and Crown Law* (1746), 315-316] ascribed the doctrine of provocation more than two centuries ago": [1978] A.C. at 717-718. His Lordship went on to suggest that juries should be directed that the reasonable man in terms of s. 3 of the Homicide Act 1957 is "a person having the power of self-control to be expected of an ordinary person of the sex and age of the accused, but in other respects sharing such of the accused's characteristics as they think would affect the gravity of the provocation to him; and that the question is not merely whether such a person would in like circumstances be provoked to lose his self-control but also whether he would react to the provocation as the accused did": at 718E-F.

It was stressed in *R.* v. *Newell* (1980) 71 Cr. App. R. 331 that the relevant special characteristic must be one which is part of the accused's personality, and not something transitory like intoxication or grief, and that there must be a connection between that characteristic and the provocation offered. The conduct complained of must have been exclusively or particularly provocative to the accused because of a characteristic marking him off from the ordinary man, whether physically or mentally, or by reason of colour, race or creed. It is not enough that the accused belonged to an excitable or violent race.

In *R.* v. *Taaka* [1982] 2 N.Z.L.R. 198 it was held that psychiatric evidence that the accused, because of his personality and background, would brood for longer than normal, and that he had an obsessive personality which was directed towards his family, was relevant to a defence of provocation to a charge of murdering a cousin whose behaviour a fortnight before he had construed as an attempt to rape his (the accused's) wife.

The objective approach has also been rejected in Ireland as illogical. The court held that in considering provocation account should be

25-38 taken of the accused's "temperament, character and circumstances": *People* v. *MacEoin* [1978] I.R. 27.

It seems to be generally agreed that drink is irrelevant, and that, as it was put in *Newell*, the jury must assume that the conduct in question was directed at a sober man: see, *e.g. R.* v. *O'Neill* [1982] V.R. 150. It has, however, been held in New Zealand that if there is evidence that a reasonable and sober man would have been provoked, the accused's intoxication may be taken into account in relation to the question of whether he was actually provoked: *R.* v. *Barton* [1977] 1 N.Z.L.R. 295.

CHAPTER 26

INVOLUNTARY CULPABLE HOMICIDE

26-12 The view of the House of Lords is that the *mens rea* required for conviction under s. 1 is the same as that for manslaughter, the only difference being perhaps that the common law offence requires a very high degree of risk: *R.* v. *Seymour (Edward)* [1983] 2 A.C. 493; see also *R.* v. *Governor of Holloway Prison, ex p. Jennings* [1983] 1 A.C. 624.

It may be, therefore, that the form of words used in *Paton* should be replaced by that in *Allan* v. *Patterson*, 1980 J.C. 57; see *infra*, para. 30-08.

26-13 See *R.* v. *Seymour (Edward)* [1983] 2 A.C. 493.

26-14 It was held in *James McRae Watson*, Criminal Appeal Court, March 1978, unreported, that the accused's fault must be a material, *i.e.* more than a minimal, cause of the accident, but that it was wrong to direct the jury that they could acquit only if they were satisfied that the whole cause was the fault of another person.

26-20 It is homicide to cause a person's death by injecting him with a dangerous drug, given the necessary degree of recklessness, even where the injection was with the consent, or at the request, of the victim: see *Finlayson* v. *H.M.A.*, 1979 J.C. 33.

26-21 *Cf.* Lord Reid in *McKendrick* v. *Sinclair*, 1972 S.C. (H.L.) 25, 54: "But culpable homicide covers a very wide variety of cases from something not far short of murder, to cases deserving little punishment. In my own experience it was not very uncommon to direct that a charge of culpable homicide should be tried summarily."

26-25 Where a weapon is produced merely to deter a potential aggressor, and is not actively brandished at him, there may be no assault by the holder of the weapon, and therefore no culpable homicide if the aggressor runs on to the weapon and is fatally injured, and this apart from any question of self-defence: *Mackenzie* v. *H.M.A.*, 1983 S.L.T. 220.

26-26   In *Mathieson* v. *H.M.A.*, 1981 S.C.C.R. 196, where death was caused by culpable and reckless fire-raising, the High Court upheld a direction to the jury that if death results directly from the commission of an unlawful act, that is culpable homicide.

In *R.* v. *Dalby* [1982] 1 W.L.R. 425 A was charged with manslaughter by supplying V with a controlled drug. A and V had each injected himself before they parted company, and V then gave himself two further injections and died in the night. It was held that A was not guilty of manslaughter by an unlawful act since that type of manslaughter requires an act directed at the victim and involving direct physical injury. There may, of course, be manslaughter by gross negligence in certain cases of this kind, more especially where the drug is administered to V by A himself: see *H.M.A.* v. *Finlayson*, 1978 S.L.T. (Notes) 18; *Finlayson* v. *H.M.A.*, 1979 J.C. 33; *cf. Khaliq* v. *H.M.A.*, 1984 S.L.T. 137.

Chapter 28

ABORTION

28-05   The protection of the Act extends to abortions carried out by nurses and others acting under the direction of, and using methods prescribed by, a medical practitioner: *Royal College of Nursing* v. *D.H.S.S.* [1981] A.C. 800.

Chapter 29

ASSAULT AND REAL INJURY

29-01   To commit an assault by setting a dog on a person one must cause the dog to move at the victim with the intention that the movement will at least frighten him: *Kay* v. *Allan*, High Court on appeal, Feb. 1978, unreported.

29-03   It may not be an assault to "present" a weapon at someone with intent to deter him from attacking the presenter, apart altogether from any question of self-defence: *Mackenzie* v. *H.M.A.*, 1983 S.L.T. 220.

29-12   The maximum penalty on any contravention of this section is nine months' imprisonment and a fine of level 5: 1975 Act, s. 289E, as inserted by Criminal Justice Act 1982, s. 54; Criminal Justice (Scotland) Act 1980, s. 57. Contraventions of this section are now often tried on indictment as additional charges by virtue of s. 457A(4) of the 1975 Act, as inserted by s. 55(1) of the Criminal Justice Act 1982, despite the fact that the maximum penalty remains as on summary conviction.

29-12   In *Skeen* v. *Shaw and Anr.*, 1979 S.L.T. (Notes) 58 the High Court pointed out that the word "hinders" had been added to the definition of the offence subsequent to *Curlett* v. *McKechnie*. They reserved their opinion as to whether hindering can be committed without a physical element, but held that even if it can not the introduction of the term "demonstrates how small a degree any physical element must be in the act of persons who place a difficulty in the way of the police." In that case the accused were charged with standing in front of and threatening constables who had a prisoner in their custody, engaging in a noisy altercation with them and making it difficult for them to get their prisoner into their van. There was, however, neither physical contact between the accused and the police nor any threat of physical violence.

For the position where the police officer is acting without warrant, see *Stirton* v. *MacPhail*, 1983 S.L.T. 34, and the commentary thereon at 1982 S.C.C.R. 307.

29-13   Section 10 of the Customs and Excise Act 1952 is repealed by the Customs and Excise Management Act 1979, and re-enacted by s. 16 of that Act.

29-21   The need to prove the accused's knowledge of the character of the complainer in a charge under s. 41 of the Police (Scotland) Act 1967 was upheld by the sheriff in *Annan* v. *Tait*, 1982 S.L.T. (Sh. Ct.) 108.

29-24   Certain cases of obtaining sexual intercourse with a woman without her consent are not rape but indecent assault: see *infra*, para. 33-21.

29-27   Section 72(2) of the Customs and Excise Act 1952 is repealed by the Customs and Excise Management Act 1979, and re-enacted by s. 85(2) of that Act.

29-29   See now Representation of the People Act 1983, s. 115(2).

29-31   For an example of excessive force by an arresting police officer, see *Bonar* v. *McLeod*, 1983 S.C.C.R. 161.

29-38   It has been held that s. 107(1) of the Mental Health (Scotland) Act 1960, which provides that no person shall be liable to criminal proceedings in respect of anything done in pursuance of the Act, applies to protect a nurse from a charge of assault by using such force as is reasonably necessary to control mentally handicapped children: *Skinner* v. *Robertson*, 1980 S.L.T. (Sh. Ct.) 43. For an example of the use of excessive force against a mental patient, in this case an adult, see *Norman* v. *Smith*, 1983 S.C.C.R. 100 in which the court made no reference to s. 107, but did refer to a departmental circular on the control of patients.

On the parent's right to prevent a teacher imposing corporal punishment, see *Campbell and Cosans* v. *United Kingdom*, Judgments and Decisions of European Court of Human Rights, Series A, Vol. 48, 25th February 1982.

Although the accused in the odd case of *Stewart* v. *Thain*, 1981 J.C. 13 was a teacher, the incident complained of took place outwith school, and he appears to have acted as the specifically appointed

29-38   agent of the child's parent who later complained about the propriety of the form of chastisement used: inducing a 15-year-old boy to remove his trousers and bend over some furniture, and then lifting the waistband of his pants and smacking him on the upper part of his buttocks. The accused was charged with indecent assault, although there was no suggestion of any sexual element, and was acquitted on the authority of *Gray* v. *Hawthorn*. It was said that humiliation might form part of a legitimate punishment.

29-39   The English Court of Appeal declined to follow the ratio of *Smart* in *Attorney-General's Reference (No. 6 of 1980)* [1981] Q.B. 715, but held that consent was not a defence to assault where there was an intention to do actual bodily harm. "Minor struggles" were said to be another matter. It was held to be irrelevant whether the assault took place in public or private. The court noted that this meant that most fights other than sporting events were illegal, but expressed the hope that their decision would not lead to unnecessary prosecutions.

29-42   For an example of an assault between rugby players, see *R.* v. *Billinghurst* [1978] Crim. L.R. 553.

29-49   Drugging may in certain circumstances be committed by supplying persons with drugs and the means for using them in the knowledge that they are to be used by the persons supplied to the danger of their health: *Khaliq* v. *H.M.A.*, 1984 S.L.T. 137; *supra*, para. 4-53.

29-52   In *Jas. McLean*, Glasgow High Court, May 1980, unreported, where there was a charge of abducting a little girl, and also a charge of raping her, Lord Kincraig directed the jury on the abduction charge that (transcript of Judge's Charge, p. 7):

> ". . . it is a crime to carry off or confine any person forcibly against their will without lawful authority. In the case of a child of six 'forcibly' is not a necessary element in the proof. It would be sufficient to constitute the crime of abducting a child if there was evidence of her being led away by the accused or inducing her to follow. That would be sufficient to establish proof that she was taken away against her will. So far as any proper authority is concerned, a stranger has no proper authority to lead away a child."

For abduction in connection with elections, see now Representation of the People Act 1983, s. 115(2)(*b*).

29-54   Add new paragraph **29-54a**:

29-54a   *Hostages.* The Taking of Hostages Act 1982, implementing the International Convention against the Taking of Hostages, provides by s. 1:

> "(1) A person, whatever his nationality, who, in the United Kingdom or elsewhere, —
> (*a*) detains any other person ('the hostage'), and
> (*b*) in order to compel a State, international governmental organisation or person to do or abstain from doing any act, threatens to kill, injure or continue to detain the hostage,
> commits an offence."

29-54a   Maximum penalty life imprisonment.

See also the Internationally Protected Persons Act 1978, s. 1(3), *infra*, para. 29-65.

29-56   In *W.* v. *H.M. Advocate*, 1982 S.C.C.R. 152 the accused was charged with culpable and reckless injury by throwing from a fifteenth-floor flat a bottle which hit someone on the ground below. He had been warned of the danger before he threw the bottle. The degree of recklessness required was said to be a total indifference to and disregard of the safety of the public.

29-60   *Khaliq* v. *H.M.A.*, 1984 S.L.T. 137 is authority for an offence of recklessly endangering the health of particular persons, in that case by causing them to sniff glue: see *supra*, para. 4-53.

In *Gizzi and Anr.* v. *Tudhope*, 1982 S.C.C.R. 442, which was a case of reckless discharge of firearms, the accused were held to be reckless in firing towards a clump of trees without considering whether there might be anyone in range behind them. *Allan* v. *Patterson*, 1980 J.C. 57, *supra*, paras. 7-70 to 7-74, was applied.

29-60   Footnote 15. Section 1 of the Guard Dogs Act 1975 provides:

> "(1) A person shall not use or permit the use of a guard dog at any premises unless a person ('the handler') who is capable of controlling the dog is present on the premises and the dog is under the control of the handler at all times while it is being so used except while it is secured so that it is not at liberty to go freely about the premises.
>
> (2) The handler of a guard dog shall keep the dog under his control at all times while it is being used as a guard dog at any premises except—
>
> > (*a*) while another handler has control over the dog; or
> >
> > (*b*) while the dog is secured so that it is not at liberty to go freely about the premises.
>
> (3) A person shall not use or permit the use of a guard dog at any premises unless a notice containing a warning that a guard dog is present is clearly exhibited at each entrance to the premises."

No offence is committed under s. 1(1) by the user of the dog where the handler is absent, provided the dog has been secured: *Rafferty* v. *Smith*, High Court on appeal, May 1978, unreported, following *Hobson* v. *Gledhill* [1978] 1 W.L.R. 215.

29-64   Add new paragraph **29-65**:

29-65   *Threats to internationally protected persons.* Section 1 of the Internationally Protected Persons Act 1978 provides, inter alia:

> "(3) If a person in the United Kingdom or elsewhere, whether a citizen of the United Kingdom and Colonies or not—
>
> > (*a*) makes to another person a threat that any person will do an act which is an offence mentioned in paragraph (*a*) of the preceding subsection; or
> >
> > (*b*) attempts to make or aids, abets, counsels or procures or is art and part in the making of such a threat to another person,
>
> with the intention that the other person shall fear that the threat will be carried out, the person who makes the threat or, as the case may be, who attempts to make it or aids, abets, counsels or procures or is art and part in

29-65 the making of it, shall in any part of the United Kingdom be guilty of an offence and liable on conviction on indictment to imprisonment for a term not exceeding ten years and not exceeding the term of imprisonment to which a person would be liable for the offence constituted by doing the act threatened at the place where the conviction occurs and at the time of the offence to which the conviction relates.

(4) For the purposes of the preceding subsections it is immaterial whether a person knows that another person is a protected person.

(5) In this section—

'act' includes omission;

'a protected person' means, in relation to an alleged offence, any of the following, namely—

(*a*) a person who at the time of the alleged offence is a Head of State, a member of a body which performs the functions of Head of State under the constitution of the State, a Head of Government or a Minister for Foreign Affairs and is outside the territory of the State in which he holds office;

(*b*) a person who at the time of the alleged offence is a representative or an official of a State or an official or agent of an international organisation of an intergovernmental character, is entitled under international law to special protection from attack on his person, freedom or dignity and does not fall within the preceding paragraph;

(*c*) a person who at the time of the alleged offence is a member of the family of another person mentioned in either of the preceding paragraphs and—

(i) if the other person is mentioned in paragraph (*a*) above, is accompanying him,

(ii) if the other person is mentioned in paragraph (*b*) above, is a member of his household;

'relevant premises' means premises at which a protected person resides or is staying or which a protected person uses for the purpose of carrying out his functions as such a person; and

'vehicle' includes any means of conveyance;

and if in any proceedings a question arises as to whether a person is or was a protected person, a certificate issued by or under the authority of the Secretary of State and stating any fact relating to the question shall be conclusive evidence of that fact."

Add new paragraph **29-66**:

29-66 *Taking hostages.* Section 1 of the Taking of Hostages Act 1982 makes it an offence to detain any other person ("the hostage") and threaten to kill, injure or detain him in order to compel a State, international governmental organisation or person to do or abstain from doing any act: maximum penalty life imprisonment: see *supra*, para. 29-54a.

CHAPTER 30

STATUTORY OFFENCES CONCERNED WITH PERSONAL INJURY

30-04 In *McQuaid* v. *Anderton* [1981] 1 W.L.R. 154 it was held that a person in the driver's seat of a towed vehicle was driving it, and *Wallace* v. *Major* was not followed.

30-07   In *Dunn* v. *Keane*, 1976 J.C. 39 it was held that the driveway from the public road to a hotel car park was a road to which the public had access, following *Harrison* v. *Hill*.

30-08   Reckless driving is now authoritatively defined in *Allan* v. *Patterson*, 1980 J.C. 57, where it was said (Lord Justice-General at 60):

> "We have no difficulty in reaching the conclusion that the Crown submission must receive effect. There is nothing in the language of section 2 as amended to suggest an intention on the part of Parliament to penalise thereunder only a course of driving embarked upon wilfully or deliberately in the face of known risks of a material kind. Inquiry into the state of knowledge of a particular driver accused of the offence created by the section as amended, and into his intention at the time, is not required at all. The statute directs attention to the quality of the driving in fact but not to the state of mind or the intention of the driver. If it were otherwise, the section, and indeed section 1, would virtually become inoperable in all but the rarest of instances. Neither is the skill or capacity of the particular driver in issue: the offence can be committed whether or not the event is followed or demonstrated by a casualty. All that is in issue and all that Parliament requires the court or the jury to consider and determine is the degree to which the driver in question falls below the standard to be expected of a careful and competent driver in all the circumstances of the particular case, and whether the degree is such as properly to attach in the judgment of court or jury the epithet or label of 'reckless.' Section 2, as its language plainly, we think, suggests, requires a judgment to be made quite objectively of a particular course of driving in proved circumstances, and what the Court or a jury has to decide, using its common sense, is whether that course of driving in these circumstances had the grave quality of recklessness. Judges and juries will readily understand, and juries might well be reminded, that before they can apply the adverb 'recklessly' to the driving in question they must find that it fell far below the standard of driving expected of the competent and careful driver and that it occurred either in the face of obvious and material dangers which were or should have been observed, appreciated and guarded against, or in circumstances which showed a complete disregard for any potential dangers which might result from the way in which the vehicle was being driven. It will be understood that in reaching a decision upon the critical issue a Judge or jury will be entitled to have regard to any explanation offered by the accused driver designed to show that his driving in the particular circumstances did not possess the quality of recklessness at the material time."

30-11   A drug in this context is "a substance which is taken into the human body by whatsoever means which does not fall within the description 'drink'. . . and which is not taken as a food, but which does affect the control of the human body": *Bradford* v. *Wilson* (1984) 78 Cr. App. R. 77, Robert Goff, L.J. at 120-121. A person suffering from the effects of glue-sniffing is therefore unfit through a drug: *ibid*; *Duffy* v. *Tudhope*, 1983 S.C.C.R. 440.

30-13   Section 25(1) of the Transport Act 1981 adds the following to the end of s. 5(3):

> "but in determining whether there was such a likelihood the court may disregard any injury to him and any damage to the vehicle."

30-14   Necessity has been held to be a defence to a charge of attempting to drive with an excess of alcohol in one's blood: *Tudhope* v. *Grubb*, 1983 S.C.C.R. 350 (Sh.Ct.); *supra*, para. 13-18.

30-15   The much litigated s. 6 is repealed by Sched. 8 to the Transport Act 1981 and replaced by the following which removes the peculiarity of the earlier provision which made the mode of proof part of the offence:

> "(1) If a person—
>   (*a*) drives or attempts to drive a motor vehicle on a road or other public place; or
>   (*b*) is in charge of a motor vehicle on a road or other public place;
> after consuming so much alcohol that the proportion of it in his breath, blood or urine exceeds the prescribed limit he shall be guilty of an offence.
>
> (2) It is a defence for a person charged with an offence under subsection (1)(*b*) above to prove that at the time he is alleged to have committed the offence the circumstances were such that there was no likelihood of his driving the vehicle whilst the proportion of alcohol in his breath, blood or urine remained likely to exceed the prescribed limit; but in determining whether there was such a likelihood the court may disregard any injury to him and any damage to the vehicle."

30-16   See also *Keane* v. *McSkimming*, 1983 S.C.C.R. 220.

30-17   See also the "Zebra" Pedestrian Crossing Regulations 1971, the duty to accord precedence being in reg. 8; "Pelican" Pedestrian Crossing Regulations and General Directions 1969, where the relevant regulation is reg. 11.

30-19   The Stage Carriages Act 1832 is repealed by the Statute Law (Repeals) Act 1981. The Burgh Police (Scotland) Act 1892 will be repealed by the Civic Government (Scotland) Act 1982.

30-20   Section 27 of the Merchant Shipping Act 1970 is amended by s. 45 of the Merchant Shipping Act 1979 so as (i) to substitute the words "of or any seaman employed in" for the words "or any member of the crew of", and (ii) to insert the words "or its machinery, navigational equipment or safety equipment" after the words "to the ship" in s. 27(1)(*a*) and also after the words "preserve the ship" in s. 27(1)(*b*).

    Section 457 of the Merchant Shipping Act 1894 is repealed by s. 44 of the Merchant Shipping Act 1979 which provides:

> "(1) If—
>   (*a*) a ship in a port in the United Kingdom; or
>   (*b*) a ship registered in the United Kingdom which is in any other port,
> is, having regard to the nature of the service for which the ship is intended, unfit by reason of the condition of the ship's hull, equipment or machinery or by reason of undermanning or by reason of overloading or improper loading to go to sea without serious danger to human life, then, subject to the following subsection, the master and the owner of the ship shall each be guilty of an offence and liable on conviction on indictment to a fine and on summary conviction to a fine not exceeding £50,000.
>   (2) It shall be a defence in proceedings for an offence under the preceding subsection to prove that at the time of the alleged offence—

30-20

    (*a*) arrangements had been made which were appropriate to ensure that before the ship went to sea it was made fit to do so without serious danger to human life by reason of the matters aforesaid which are specified in the charge; or

    (*b*) it was reasonable not to have made such arrangements."

30-21   In order to obtain a conviction under this section, the Crown must show that a potential danger to persons passing along the railway existed as the result of the accused's negligence: *Rodger* v. *Smith*, 1981 S.L.T. (Notes) 31.

30-22   The Air Navigation Order 1976 is repealed by the Air Navigation Order 1980, and Articles 44 to 46 of the 1976 Order are replaced by Articles 45 to 47 of the 1980 Order, with the substitution of "recklessly" for "wilfully".

Section 11 of the Civil Aviation Act 1949 is repealed by the Civil Aviation Act 1982, and re-enacted by s. 81 of that Act.

30-23   The Protection of Aircraft Act 1973 is repealed by the Aviation Security Act 1982. Section 1 of the 1973 Act is now s. 2 of the 1982 Act; the power to direct searches, etc. is now in s. 13 of that Act. Section 16 of the 1973 Act is now s. 4 of the 1982 Act.

Section 2 of the 1973 Act is now s. 3 of the 1982 Act, subject to some insignificant verbal changes.

30-26   Section 1 of the Firearms Act 1982 applies the Firearms Act 1968 to any imitation firearm which has the appearance of being a firearm to which s. 1 of the 1968 Act applies, if it is so constructed or adapted as to be readily convertible into a firearm to which that section applies, *i.e.* if it can be so converted without any special skill on the part of the person converting it in the construction or adaptation of any kind of firearm, and the conversion work involved does not require equipment or tools other than such as are in common use by persons carrying on works of construction and maintenance in their own homes. In the application of the 1982 Act, s. 57(1) of the 1968 Act is to be read without paras. (*b*) and (*c*). The provisions of s. 4(3) and (4) of the 1968 Act do not apply to imitation firearms to which the 1982 Act applies: 1982 Act, s. 2(2). In addition, the 1982 Act does not operate to apply to imitation firearms the provisions of the 1968 Act relating to, or to the enforcement of control over, the manner in which a firearm is used or the circumstances in which it is carried, but this is without prejudice to the application of these provisions to imitation firearms independently of the 1982 Act.

Kelly v. *MacKinnon*, 1983 S.L.T. 9, which held that the fact that a replica revolver and a starting pistol which had been rendered incapable of firing were easily convertible so as to be capable of being fired did not make them firearms, must now be applied subject to the Firearms Act 1982.

Footnote 27. Add: *R.* v. *Burke* (1978) 67 Cr. App. R. 220. The view has been expressed that it is unlikely that any firearm made in this century will be regarded as an antique: *Bennett* v. *Brown* (1980) 71 Cr. App. R. 109.

30-27   The offence is one of strict liability, and it is immaterial that the accused does not know that what he has is a firearm: *R.* v. *Hussain* [1981] 1 W.L.R. 416.

A rifle whose rifling has been removed so as to make it a smooth bore gun does not require a firearms certificate: *R.* v. *Hucklebridge* [1980] 1 W.L.R. 1284.

30-31   Where a weapon has been so adapted that by reason of its modified design it can fire only single shots, it does not come within s. 5: *R.* v. *Jobling* [1981] Crim. L.R. 625; *cf. Kelly* v. *MacKinnon*, 1983 S.L.T. 9; *supra*, para. 30-26. Possession of all the parts of a stripped down prohibited weapon is possession of the weapon: *R.* v. *Pannell* (1982) 76 Cr. App. R. 53.

30-35   It has been held that it is not necessary to prove that at some time before its actual use the firearm was being carried with the intention of using it, and that the ratio of such cases as *R.* v. *Jura* [1954] 1 Q.B. 503 (para. 30-46 in the main work) does not apply to section 18: *R.* v. *Houghton (Andrew)* [1982] Crim. L.R. 112.

Footnote 41. Delete the references to the Vagrancy Act and the Prevention of Crimes Act and substitute Civic Government (Scotland) Act 1982, s. 57.

30-36   The possession of a shotgun certificate is not lawful authority within s. 19: *Ross* v. *Collins* [1982] Crim. L.R. 368; but it has been held that the exercise of a public right of recreation on the foreshore is: *McLeod* v. *McLeod*, 1982 S.C.C.R. 130 (Sh. Ct.).

30-39   Section 4 of the Vagrancy Act 1824 is repealed by the Civic Government (Scotland) Act 1982.

30-40   Where consecutive sentences are imposed, the relevant period under s. 21 is that of their aggregate: *Davies* v. *Tomlinson* (1980) 71 Cr. App. R. 279.

30-44   A flick knife is a weapon made for use for causing personal injury: *Tudhope* v. *O'Neill*, 1982 S.C.C.R. 45; *cf. Gibson* v. *Wales* [1983] 1 W.L.R. 393: *R.* v. *Simpson (Calvin)* [1983] 1 W.L.R. 1494. So, too, are nunchaca sticks: *Hemming* v. *Annan*, 1982 S.C.C.R. 432.

Intention to cause personal injury is a question of fact which can be inferred from the general circumstances of the accused's possession: *Lopez* v. *MacNab*, 1978 J.C. 41. It has been held in England that intention to cause injury does not include an intention to intimidate unless it is accompanied by an intention to injure by shock: *R.* v. *Rapier* (1979) 70 Cr. App. R. 17. See also *R.* v. *Williamson* (1977) 67 Cr. App. R. 35.

30-45   What constitutes a reasonable excuse is a question of fact for the trial court: compare *Hemming* v. *Annan*, 1982 S.C.C.R. 432 and *Kincaid* v. *Tudhope*, 1983 S.C.C.R. 389.

30-46   *Ohlson* was applied in *Bates* v. *Bulman* [1979] 1 W.L.R. 1190 where

30-46 the accused, after punching a man, requested and received from a friend a clasp knife which he opened and held against the victim's head.

Add new paragraph **30-46a**:

30-46a *Obstructing search for weapons.* Section 4(1) of the Criminal Justice (Scotland) Act 1980 gives a police constable power to search persons he has reasonable cause to suspect of having offensive weapons, and s. 4(2) provides:

> "Any person who—
> (a) intentionally obstructs a constable in the exercise of the constable's powers under subsection (1) above; or
> (b) conceals from a constable acting in the exercise of the said powers an offensive weapon,
> shall be guilty of an offence and liable on summary conviction to a fine not exceeding [level 3 on the standard scale]."

It is not an offence under s. 4(2)(*b*) for a person in possession of a weapon to hand it to a friend on the approach of the police: *Burke* v. *Mackinnon*, 1983 S.C.C.R. 23.

30-47 Section 4 of the Vagrancy Act is repealed by the Civic Government (Scotland) Act 1982. Section 73 of the Customs and Excise Act 1952 is now s. 86 of the Customs and Excise Management Act 1979.

30-50 Although no cases or information have been prescribed under subs. 3(3), failure to give information may be an offence under s. 3(1) where the information is necessary to prevent exposure to risk to health or safety: *Carmichael* v. *Rosehall Engineering Works Ltd.*, 1983 S.C.C.R. 353; *R.* v. *Swan Hunter Shipbuilders Ltd.*, [1981] I.C.R. 831.

On the relationship between s. 3 and s. 4, see *Aitchison* v. *Howard Doris Ltd.*, 1979 S.L.T. (Notes) 22.

CHAPTER 31

OFFENCES AGAINST CHILDREN

31-04 It has been held in the House of Lords that the offence of wilful neglect requires intention or at least recklessness: *R.* v. *Sheppard* [1981] A.C. 394. Where what is in issue is failure to provide medical aid the prosecution must therefore show either that the parent was aware of the risk or that the parent's unawareness was due to his not caring whether the child's health was at risk or not: Lord Diplock at 403 A.

The matter has not been reconsidered in Scotland since *Sheppard*, so that the law remains as laid down in *R.* v. *Senior* [1899] 1 Q.B. 283 and *Clark* v. *H.M. Advocate*, 1968 J.C. 53: *c.f.* Lord Fraser of Tullybelton's dissenting speech in *Sheppard* at 416 to 417.

31-13 Add new paragraph **31-14**:

31-14 *Indecent photographs.* It is an offence to take or permit to be taken

31-14 any indecent photograph of a person under the age of 16: Civic Government (Scotland) Act 1982, s. 52: maximum penalty two years' imprisonment and a fine on indictment; see *infra*, para. 41-22a.

CHAPTER 32

CRUELTY TO ANIMALS

32-01 Footnote 4. An order of disqualification made under the Protection of Animals (Amendment) Act 1954 which refers to having the custody of cattle is to be interpreted as extending to sheep: *Wastie* v. *Phillips* [1972] 1 W.L.R. 1293

32-02 It was held in *Patchett* v. *MacDougall*, 1983 S.C.C.R. 361 that it is not necessarily cruelty to kill an animal by shooting it at point-blank range.

32-09 These Acts are repealed and replaced by the Wildlife and Countryside Act 1981.

CHAPTER 33

RAPE

33-03
33-04 There is English authority that a person who is born of a particular sex and remains biologically of that sex is a person of that sex even if he has undergone a sex-change operation: *R.* v. *Tan* [1983] Q.B. 1053.

33-06 It seems clear now that the crime here is indecent assault: *Sweeney and Anr.* v. *X*, 1982 S.C.C.R. 509.

33-09 Where the woman is under the influence of drink the degree of violence required may be less than in the case of a sober woman: *Sweeney and Anr.* v. *X*, 1982 S.C.C.R. 509.

Add new paragraph **33-09a**:

33-09a *Error.* A mistaken but genuine belief that the woman is a consenting party is a defence to rape: *Meek and Ors.* v. *H.M.A.*, 1982 S.C.C.R. 613, and see commentary thereon; *R.* v. *Morgan* [1976] A.C. 182; *cf. Pappajohn* v. *The Queen* [1980] 2 S.C.R. 121. It is not necessary for the judge to direct the jury on this matter where the defence case is that the woman actively co-operated and the Crown case is that she struggled: *ibid.*; the point was not taken in *Sweeney and Anr.* v. *X*, 1982 S.C.C.R. 509. For recent English cases on recklessness in this matter, which apparently occupies a special position in English law (which, in view of *Meek*, *supra*, may also apply in Scotland), see *R.*

33-09a v. *Pigg* [1982] 1 W.L.R. 762; *R.* v. *Satnam S.* (1984) 78 Cr. App. R. 149.

It has been held in New Zealand that if the accused initially believes the woman is consenting, but realises after penetration that this is not the case and carries on nonetheless, he is guilty of rape: *R.* v. *Kaitamaki* [1984] 3 W.L.R. 137.

An error resulting from intoxication has been held to be irrelevant: *R.* v. *Woods* (1981) 74 Cr. App. R. 312; *Leary* v. *The Queen* [1978] 1 S.C.R. 29.

33-10 "The important matter is not the amount of resistance put up but whether the woman remained an unwilling party throughout. The significance of resistance is only as evidence of unwillingness": *H.M.A.* v. *Barbour*, 1982 S.C.C.R. 195, Lord Stewart at 198; *cf. R.* v. *Olugboja* [1982] Q.B. 320.

33-12 It has now been held that a husband can be guilty of raping his wife,
33-13 at least where the parties are living separately: *H.M.A.* v. *Duffy*, 1983 S.L.T. 7.

33-16 The definition of "defective" is repealed by the Mental Health
to (Amendment) (Scotland) Act 1983. The words "a defective" are
33-18 replaced wherever they occur by "protected by the provisions of this section", and s. 96(6A) defines a protected person as a woman "suffering from a state of arrested or incomplete development of mind which includes significant impairment of intelligence and social functioning": Mental Health (Amendment) (Scotland) Act 1983, s. 5(3).

33-19 Section 80(4) of the Criminal Justice (Scotland) Act 1980 applies s. 97 of the Mental Health (Scotland) Act 1960 to homosexual acts, *i.e.* sodomy or gross indecency between males.

33-21 It seems to be clear from *Sweeney and Anr.* v. *X*, 1982 S.C.C.R. 509 that to have intercourse with a woman who has made herself so drunk as to be incapable of consent is indecent assault, and the position should be the same where the woman is asleep. Clandestine injury is thus just another name for an indecent assault involving penetration.

CHAPTER 34

SODOMY AND BESTIALITY

34-01 Sodomy in private between consenting men over the age of twenty-one is legalised by s. 80 of the Criminal Justice (Scotland) Act 1980: see *infra*, para. 36-17.

OTHER SEXUAL OFFENCES

36-14   Section 4 of the Vagrancy Act 1824 is repealed by the Civic Government (Scotland) Act 1982.

36-15   *Cf. Niven* v. *Tudhope*, 1982 S.C.C.R. 365.

36-17   Homosexual offences are now governed by s. 80 of the Criminal
36-18   Justice (Scotland) Act 1980 whose general effect is that homosexual conduct between consenting males over the age of 21 in private is not criminal; it does not even constitute the common law crime of shameless indecency. Section 7 of the Sexual Offences (Scotland) Act 1976 is repealed by the Act of 1980. Section 80 of the Act of 1980 provides, inter alia:

> "(1) Subject to the provisions of this section, a homosexual act in private shall not be an offence provided that the parties consent thereto and have attained the age of twenty-one years.
> (2) An act which would otherwise be treated for the purposes of this Act as being done in private shall not be so treated if done—
>> (*a*) when more than two persons take part or are present or
>> (*b*) in a lavatory to which the public have, or are permitted to have, access whether on payment or otherwise . . .
> (5) Subsection (1) above shall not prevent a homosexual act from being an offence under any provision of the Army Act 1955, the Air Force Act 1955 or the Naval Discipline Act 1957.
> (6) In this section, 'a homosexual act' means sodomy or an act of gross indecency by one male person with another male person."

The effect of these provisions is that homosexual behaviour which is not protected by them remains a crime at common law, whether it is sodomy or some lesser form of gross indecency between males which would be prosecuted as shameless indecency or, in cases involving young boys, as lewd practices: see para. 36-09 in the main work.

It is also an offence, under s. 80(7), to commit or be party to, or to procure or attempt to procure, the commission of a homosexual act in any of the following cases:

> "(*a*) otherwise than in private;
> (*b*) without the consent of both parties to the act;
> (*c*) with a person under the age of twenty-one years; or
> (*d*) where the act is committed on board a United Kingdom merchant ship, wherever it may be, by a male person who is a member of the crew of that ship with another male person who is a member of the crew of that ship or any other United Kingdom merchant ship."

"Member of the crew" includes the master of the ship, and a "United Kingdom merchant ship" is one registered in the United Kingdom and habitually used or used at the time of the offence for carrying passengers or goods for reward: s. 80(8).

The maximum penalty where the charge is brought under s. 80(7) is

36-18   two years' imprisonment and a fine on indictment, three months or a fine on summary conviction: (s. 80(10)), proceedings must be commenced not later than twelve months after the offence: s. 80(14).

It is a defence to a charge under s. 80(7)(*c*), where the accused is under 24 years of age and has not been previously charged with a like offence, that he had reasonable cause to believe the other person was aged 21 or over: s. 80(11); *cf.* paras. 36-03 *et seq.* in the main work.

Male persons who are mentally handicapped are protected by section 80(3) which provides:

> "A male person who is suffering from mental [handicap] which is of such a nature or degree that he is incapable of living an independent life or of guarding himself against serious exploitation cannot in law give any consent which, by virtue of subsection (1) above, would prevent a homosexual act from being an offence; but a person shall not be convicted on account of the incapacity of such a male person to consent, of an offence consisting of such an act if he proves that he did not know and had no reason to suspect that male person to be suffering from such mental [handicap]."

In addition s. 97 of the Mental Health (Scotland) Act 1960 applies to sodomy or gross indecency between males: Criminal Justice (Scotland) Act 1980, s. 80(4).

36-20
36-21   Shameless indecency has recently been revived and extended to the sale or display of obscene articles: see *infra*, para. 41-16.

36-22   To present a show of obscene films to a group of men constitutes shameless indecency, provided that more than two men in all are present: see *supra*, para. 36-17; *Watt* v. *Annan*, 1978 J.C. 84.

36-24   Section 380 of the Burgh Police (Scotland) Act 1892 is repealed by the Civic Government (Scotland) Act 1982.

36-25   Premises to which people resort for sodomy or other acts of gross indecency between males in circumstances in which resort thereto for heterosexual acts would make them a brothel are to be treated as a brothel for the purposes of s. 13: Criminal Justice (Scotland) Act 1980, s. 80(13).

36-26   See Leno, "De Lustris", 1979 S.L.T. (News) 73.

In *Kelly* v. *Purvis* [1983] Q.B. 663, where the premises in question were a massage parlour in which the masseuses offered an extra masturbation service for fees payable directly to them, it was held that any premises where more than one woman offered to participate in physical acts of indecency for the sexual gratification of men was a brothel. It does not matter that sexual intercourse is not provided, and it was said that it would also not matter if no charge was made by the women concerned: *cf. Winter* v. *Woolfe* [1931] 1 K.B. 549.

36-28   Section 403 of the Burgh Police (Scotland) Act 1892 is repealed by the Civic Government (Scotland) Act 1982.

36-29   Including a male brothel: Criminal Justice (Scotland) Act 1980, s.

36-29   80(13); *supra*, para. 36-25.

36-32   The term mental defective is removed by the Mental Health (Amendment) (Scotland) Act 1982, and the section is applied to protect women "suffering from a state of arrested or incomplete development of mind which includes significant impairment of intelligence and social functioning": s. 96(6A), inserted by Mental Health (Amendment) (Scotland) Act 1983, s. 5(3).

Add new paragraph **36-32a**:

36-32a   *Procuring males*. It is an offence to procure or attempt to procure the commission of a homosexual act contrary to s. 80(7) of the Criminal Justice (Scotland) Act 1980: *supra*, para. 36-17.

It is also an offence contrary to section 80(9) of that Act to procure or attempt to procure the commission of a homosexual act between two other male persons: maximum penalty as for s. 80(7); *supra*, para. 36-17.

36-38   Mental defectives are now known as mentally handicapped persons: Mental Health (Amendment) (Scotland) Act 1983, s. 5(1). For a definition of the persons protected by s. 96 of the Mental Health (Scotland) Act 1960, see *supra*, para. 36-32.

36-40   Footnote 10. Add: *Smith* v. *Sellers*, 1978 J.C. 79.

36-41   Section 381(22) and (23) of the Burgh Police (Scotland) Act 1892 is repealed as a result of being replaced by s. 46 of the Civic Government (Scotland) Act 1982 which provides:

> "(1) A prostitute (whether male or female) who for the purposes of prostitution—
> (*a*) loiters in a public place:
> (*b*) solicits in a public place or in any other place so as to be seen from a public place; or
> (*c*) importunes any person who is in a public place,
> shall be guilty of an offence and liable, on summary conviction, to a fine not exceeding [level 2 on the standard scale].
> (2) In subsection (1) above, 'public place' has the same meaning as in section 133 of this Act but includes—
> (*a*) any place to which at the material time the public are permitted to have access, whether on payment or otherwise; and
> (*b*) any public conveyance other than a taxi or hire car within the meaning of section 23 of this Act."

"Public place" is defined in s. 133 as follows:

> "'public place' means any plac? (whether a thoroughfare or not) to which the public have unrestricted access and includes—
> (*a*) the doorways or entrances of premises abutting on any such place; and
> (*b*) any common passage, close, court, stair, garden or yard pertinent to any tenement or group of separately owned houses."

Section 23 provides, inter alia:

> "(1) . . .
> 'taxi' means a hire car which is engaged, by arrangements made in public

36-41

place between the person to be conveyed in it (or a person acting on his behalf) and its driver for a journey beginning there and then; and

'private hire car' means a hire car other than a taxi within the meaning of this subsection.

(2) In subsection (1) above, 'hire car' means a motor vehicle with a driver (other than a vehicle being a public service vehicle within the meaning of section 1(1)(*a*) of the Public Passenger Vehicles Act 1981) which is, with a view to profit, available for hire by the public for personal conveyance."

Section 80(12) of the Criminal Justice (Scotland) Act 1980 provides:

"A person who knowingly lives wholly or in part on the earnings of another from male prostitution or who solicits or importunes any male person for the purpose of procuring the commission of a homosexual act within the meaning of subsection (6) above shall be liable:

(*a*) on summary conviction to imprisonment for a term not exceeding six months; or

(*b*) on conviction on indictment to imprisonment for a term not exceeding two years."

For the meaning of "a homosexual act", see *supra*, para. 36-17.

See also C. Gane, "Soliciting for Immoral Purposes", 1978 S.L.T. (News) 181.

36-43 Maximum penalty for a contravention of s. 12(1)(*a*) of the Sexual Offences (Scotland) Act 1976 is the same as for s. 12(1)(*b*): para. 36-41 in the main work.

36-46 In *R.* v. *Farrugia (Francis)* (1979) 69 Cr. App. R. 108 taxi drivers waited at an escort agency where they also collected prostitutes and took them to hotels and there introduced them to the agency's clients. They were paid only their normal fare but they collected an agency fee from the client which they delivered to the agency, £5 of which was received by some of the girls. The girls did not pay any of their own earnings to the agency. The drivers, as well as the persons running the agency, were convicted of living on the earnings of prostitution.

36-48 See also *R.* v. *Calderhead* (1979) 68 Cr. App. R. 37.

CHAPTER 37

TREASON AND ALLIED OFFENCES

37-53 The death penalty is removed by the Armed Forces Act 1981, Sched. 5, Pt. II.

37-57 Maximum penalty now a fine of level 4: Legal Aid Act 1979, Sched. 1.

The words "committee, court, tribunal or other" are inserted before "any" in proviso (i): *ibid*.

37-58 Footnote 8. Section 17 of the Ministry of Supply Act 1939 is repealed by the Supply Powers Act 1975 and replaced by s. 5 of that Act; s. 80 of the Agriculture Act 1947 is repealed by the Agricultural Statistics Act 1979 and replaced by s. 3 of that Act; the Cinematograph Films Act 1957 is repealed by the Film Levy Finance Act 1981, and s. 5 is replaced by s. 8 of that Act.

CHAPTER 38

OFFENCES OF DISHONESTY AGAINST THE STATE

38-01   The Customs and Excise Act 1952 has been largely repealed by and re-enacted in the Customs and Excise Management Act 1979, "the 1979 Act."

38-02   This section is now replaced by s. 170 of the 1979 Act which, as amended by s. 23 of the Forgery and Counterfeiting Act 1981, provides:

"(1) Without prejudice to any other provision of the Customs and Excise Acts 1979, if any person—
(a) knowingly acquires possession of any of the following goods, that is to say—
(i) goods which have been unlawfully removed from a warehouse or Queen's warehouse;
(ii) goods which are chargeable with a duty which has not been paid;
(iii) goods with respect to the importation or exportation of which any prohibition or restriction is for the time being in force under or by virtue of any enactment; or
(b) is in any way knowingly concerned in carrying, removing, depositing, harbouring, keeping or concealing or in any manner dealing with any such goods,
and does so with intent to defraud Her Majesty of any duty payable on the goods or to evade any such prohibition or restriction with respect to the goods he shall be guilty of an offence under this section and may be detained.
(2) Without prejudice to any other provision of the Customs and Excise Acts 1979, if any person is, in relation to any goods, in any way knowingly concerned in any fraudulent evasion or attempt at evasion—
(a) of any duty chargeable on the goods;
(b) of any prohibition or restriction for the time being in force with respect to the goods under or by virtue of any anactment; or
(c) of any provision of the Customs and Excise Acts 1979 applicable to the goods,
he shall be guilty of an offence under this section and may be detained.
(3) Subject to subsection (4) or (4A) below, a person guilty of an offence under this section shall be liable—
(a) on summary conviction, to a penalty of the prescribed sum or of three times the value of the goods, whichever is the greater, or to imprisonment for a term not exceeding 6 months, or to both; or
(b) on conviction on indictment, to a penalty of any amount, or to imprisonment for a term not exceeding 2 years, or to both.
(4) In the case of an offence under this section in connection with a

prohibition or restriction on importation or exportation having effect by virtue of section 3 of the Misuse of Drugs Act 1971, subsection (3) above shall have effect subject to the modifications specified in Schedule 1 to this Act.

(4A) In the case of an offence under this section in connection with the prohibitions contained in sections 20 and 21 of the Forgery and Counterfeiting Act 1981, subsection (3)(*b*) above shall have effect as if for the words '2 years' there were substituted the words '10 years'.

(5) In any case where a person would, apart from this subsection, be guilty of—

(*a*) an offence under this section in connection with a prohibition or restriction; and

(*b*) a corresponding offence under the enactment or other instrument imposing the prohibition or restriction, being an offence for which a fine or other penalty is expressly provided by that enactment or other instrument,

he shall not be guilty of the offence mentioned in paragraph (*a*) of this subsection."

Cf. R. v. *Whitehead* [1982] Q.B. 1272.

Sections 20 and 21 of the Forgery and Counterfeiting Act 1981 refer to the importation and exportation of counterfeit notes and coins.

"Fraudulently" in s. 170(2) requires proof of dishonest conduct deliberately intended to evade the prohibition, restriction or duty, but does not require proof of an act of deceit in presence of a customs officer. A failure to stop a car when signalled to do so by a police officer is therefore sufficient if done with the necessary intent: *Att.-Gen's Reference (No. 1 of 1981)* [1982] Q.B. 848; see also *R.* v. *Jakeman* (1982) 76 Cr. App. R. 223.

Merely to deal in prohibited goods, such as drugs, which must at some time have been illegally imported does not in itself show an intent to evade the prohibition — there must be a nexus between the dealing and the importation: *R.* v. *Watts and Stack* (1979) 70 Cr. App. R. 187.

An insurance company which pays out on a policy for the theft of goods where the goods are known to be uncustomed is not guilty of a breach of s. 170, but such a payment is *contra bonos mores* and there is no obligation on the company to make it: *Geismar* v. *Sun Alliance Ltd.* [1978] 1 Q.B. 383.

"Evade" means only "avoid or get round", and a person who believes he is acting legally can act with intent to evade a prohibition: *R.* v. *Hurford-Jones* (1977) 65 Cr. App. R. 263, a case under what is now s. 68(2) of the 1979 Act — being knowingly concerned in the export of goods with intent to evade a prohibition.

In *R.* v. *Taaffe* [1984] 2 W.L.R. 326 it was held that the prosecution must show that the accused knew the goods were subject to a prohibition; and that where he believed that what were in fact drugs was currency, and also mistakenly believed that currency was subject to a prohibition, he had committed no offence. See also *R.* v. *Hennessy (Timothy)* (1978) 68 Cr. App. R. 419.

Footnote 9. Section 290(2) is now s. 154(2) of the 1979 Act.

Section 70 is now replaced by s. 83 of the 1979 Act which provides:

"(1) Where, in pursuance of any power conferred by the customs and

38-03   excise Acts or of any requirement imposed by or under those Acts, a seal, lock or mark is used to secure or identify any goods for any of the purposes of those Acts and—

(a) at any time while the goods are in the United Kingdom or within the limits of any port or on passage between ports in the United Kingdom, the seal, lock or mark is wilfully and prematurely removed or tampered with by any person; or

(b) at any time before the seal, lock or mark is lawfully removed, any of the goods are wilfully removed by any person,

that person and the person then in charge of the goods shall each be liable on summary conviction to a penalty of [level 5 on the standard scale].

(2) For the purposes of subsection (1) above, goods in a ship or aircraft shall be deemed to be in the charge of the master of the ship or commander of the aircraft.

(3) Where, in pursuance of any Community requirement or practice which relates to the movement of goods between countries or of any international agreement to which the United Kingdom is a party and which so relates,—

(a) a seal, lock or mark is used (whether in the United Kingdom or elsewhere) to secure or identify any goods for customs or excise purposes; and

(b) at any time while the goods are in the United Kingdom, the seal, lock or mark is wilfully and prematurely removed or tampered with by any person, that person and the person then in charge of the goods shall each be liable on summary conviction to a penalty of [level 5 of the standard scale]."

Footnote 10. The definition is now in s. 1(1) of the 1979 Act.

38-04   Section 71 is re-enacted by s. 84 of the 1979 Act with some verbal amendments. The offence is committed whether or not the intended recipient is in a position to receive the message or is actually engaged in smuggling at the time: s. 84(3). It is for the accused to prove that any signal was not connected with smuggling: s. 84(4). The offence is specifically made a summary offence.

38-05   Section 72 is now s. 85 of the 1979 Act. Breach of subs. (1) is made a summary offence punishable by a fine of level 1.

Footnotes 12, 14. The definition is now in s. 1(1) of the 1979 Act.

38-06   Section 73 is now re-enacted by s. 86 of the 1979 Act, with the replacement of "customs Acts" by "any provision of the customs and excise Acts relating to imported goods or prohibited or restricted goods". The "customs and excise Acts" are the 1979 Act, the other Acts of 1979 relating to duties (cc. 3 to 7 inclusive), and any other enactment for the time being in force relating to customs and excise.

38-07   Section 74 is now s. 87 of the 1979 Act. A contravention of the section is a summary offence: maximum penalty a fine of level 3.

38-08   The relevant provisions are now ss. 167 to 169 of the 1979 Act.

38-09   Section 301 is replaced by s. 167 of the 1979 Act, which, as applied to Scotland by s. 175(1)(b) of that Act, provides:

38-09   "(1) If any person either knowingly or recklessly—

(*a*)   makes or signs, or causes to be made or signed, or delivers or causes to be delivered to the Commissioners or an officer, any declaration, notice, certificate or other document whatsoever; or

(*b*)   makes any statement in answer to any question put to him by an officer which he is required by or under any enactment to answer,

being a document or statement produced or made for any purpose of any assigned matter, which is untrue in any material particular, he shall be guilty of an offence under this subsection and may be detained; and any goods in relation to which the document or statement was made shall be liable to forfeiture.

(2) Without prejudice to subsection (4) below, a person who commits an offence under subsection (1) above shall be liable—

(*a*)   on summary conviction, to a penalty of the prescribed sum, or to imprisonment for a term not exceeding 6 months, or to both; or

(*b*)   on conviction on indictment, to a penalty of any amount, or to imprisonment for a term not exceeding 2 years, or to both.

(3) If any person—

(*a*)   makes or signs, or causes to be made or signed, or delivers or causes to be delivered to the Commissioners or an officer, any declaration, notice, certificate or other document whatsoever; or

(*b*)   makes any statement in answer to any question put to him by an officer which he is required by or under any enactment to answer,

being a document or statement produced or made for any purpose of any assigned matter, which is untrue in any material particular, then, without prejudice to subsection (4) below, he shall be liable on summary conviction to a penalty of [level 4 on the standard scale].

(4) Where by reason of any such document or statement as is mentioned in subsection (1) or (3) above the full amount of any duty payable is not paid or any overpayment is made in respect of any drawback, allowance, rebate or repayment of duty, the amount of the duty unpaid or of the overpayment shall be recoverable as a debt due to the Crown or may be recovered as a civil debt."

Footnote 15. See now s. 170; *supra*, para. 38-02.

38-10   Section 302 is now s. 168 of the 1979 Act: maximum penalty two years' imprisonment and a fine on indictment, six months and a fine on summary conviction.

38-11   Section 303 is now s. 169 of the 1979 Act. Breach of s. 169 is specifically made a summary offence. The offence of hindering or deceiving an officer may be committed before, during or after the weighing, etc.

Footnote 16. Section 271 is now s. 136 of the 1979 Act.

38-12   Footnote 17. Section 44 is now s. 49 of the 1979 Act.

38-13   Section 45 is re-enacted with some verbal alterations in s. 50 of the 1979 Act: maximum penalty a fine and two years' imprisonment on indictment, six months and the prescribed sum or three times the value

38-13   of the goods, whichever is the greater on summary conviction, for offences under what was formerly s. 45(1) of the Act of 1952 and is now s. 50(2) or (3) of the 1979 Act. Where the offence relates to a prohibition or restriction having effect by virtue of s. 3 of the Misuse of Drugs Act 1971 penalties are as for contraventions of the latter Act. Maximum penalty for offences under what was formerly s. 45(2) of the Act of 1952 and is now s. 50(6) of the 1979 Act is a fine of level 3 or three times the value of the goods, whichever is the greater. Where an offence under s. 50(2) or (3) relates to counterfeit currency or coin, the maximum penalty is ten years' imprisonment.

Section 50(7) provides:

> "In any case where a person would, apart from this subsection, be guilty of—
> (*a*)   an offence under this section in connection with the importation of goods contrary to a prohibition or restriction; and
> (*b*)   a corresponding offence under the enactment or other instrument imposing the prohibition or restriction, being an offence for which a fine or other penalty is expressly provided by that enactment or other instrument,
> he shall not be guilty of the offence mentioned in paragraph (*a*) of this subsection."

Cf. R. v. *Whitehead* [1982] Q.B. 1272, a case under s. 304 of the Act of 1952.

38-14   Section 55 is re-enacted with some verbal alterations in s. 67 of the 1979 Act. Breach of s. 67 is specifically made a summary offence.

38-15   Section 7 is replaced by s. 13 of the 1979 Act. The new section gives a specific power of detention.

38-16   Section 9 is replaced by s. 15 of the 1979 Act, breach of which is specifically made a summary offence, for which the offender may be detained.

38-17   Section 10 is replaced by s. 16 of the 1979 Act. Section 16(3) provides that any person committing or aiding or abetting the commission of an offence under the section may be detained.

Footnote 21. Section 56 of the Pipe-lines Act 1962 is repealed by the 1979 Act and re-enacted by s. 162 of that Act.

38-18   Section 92 is now s. 100 of the 1979 Act. Breach of subs. (1) is specifically made a summary offence.

Removal, etc. of goods liable to forfeiture is now an indictable offence with a maximum penalty of any amount and two years' imprisonment: maximum penalty on summary conviction six months and a fine of the prescribed sum or three times the value of the goods, whichever is the greater.

Footnote 22. See now s. 92 of the 1979 Act.

38-19   Section 98 is now s. 17 of the Alcoholic Liquor Duties Act 1979,

38-19   breach of which is an indictable offence with a maximum penalty of any amount and two years' imprisonment: maximum penalty on summary conviction is six months and the prescribed sum or three times the value of the goods, whichever is the greater.

38-21   Section 38(1) of the Finance Act 1972 is repealed by the Value Added Tax Act 1983 and replaced by s. 39(1) of that Act.

Section 39(2) of the Value Added Tax Act 1983 makes it an offence,

> "If any person—
> (*a*) with intent to deceive produces, furnishes or sends for the purposes of this Act or otherwise makes use for those purposes of any document which is false in a material particular; or
> (*b*) in furnishing any information for the purposes of this Act makes any statement which he knows to be false in a material particular or recklessly makes a statement which is false in a material particular."

Maximum penalty two years' imprisonment and a penalty of any amount on indictment, six months and the prescribed sum on summary conviction.

There is also a blanket provision in s. 39(3) of the Act which provides:

> "Where a person's conduct during any specified period must have involved the commission by him of one or more offences under the preceding provisions of this section, then, whether or not the particulars of that offence or those offences are known, he shall, by virtue of this subsection, be guilty of an offence and liable—
> (*a*) on summary conviction, to a penalty of the statutory maximum or, if greater, three times the amount of any tax that was or was intended to be evaded by his conduct, or to imprisonment for a term not exceeding 6 months or to both; or
> (*b*) on conviction on indictment, to a penalty of any amount or to imprisonment for a term not exceediing 2 years or to both."

What might be called reset of untaxed goods is dealt with by s. 39(4) of the Act which provides:

> "If any person acquires possession of or deals with any goods, or accepts the supply of any services, having reason to believe that tax on the supply of the goods or services or on the importation of the goods has been or will be evaded, he shall be liable on summary conviction to a penalty of level 5 on the standard scale or three times the amount of the tax, whichever is the greater."

38-22   The Representation of the People Act 1949 is repealed and re-enacted by the Representation of the People Act 1983, "the 1983 Act."

38-23   Corrupt practices other than personation are punishable on indictment by one year's imprisonment or a fine, and on conviction in a summary court by three months and the prescribed sum, or in an election court by a fine or the prescribed sum: 1983 Act, s. 168.

The requirement for trial by the sheriff principal is now in s. 172(3) of the 1983 Act.

38-24   Section 140(3) is now s. 169(4) of the 1983 Act. Section 139 is now s. 159 of the Act.
Footnote 26. Section 151(*a*) is now s. 173(*a*) of the 1983 Act.
Footnote 27. Section 152 is now s. 174 of the 1983 Act.

38-25   Footnote 28. Section 141(1) is now s. 161 of the 1983 Act. The Election Commissioners Act was repealed by the Representation of the People Act 1969.
Footnote 29. Section 141(2) is now s. 162 of the 1983 Act.

38-26   Section 47 is now s. 60 of the 1983 Act.
Footnote 30. Section 168(2) is now s. 190 of the 1983 Act.

38-27   Section 63 is now s. 75 of the 1983 Act.
Footnote 34. *D.P.P.* v. *Luft* is now reported at [1977] A.C. 962.

38-28   Section 70 is now s. 82 of the 1983 Act.
Footnote 35. Section 73(1) is now s. 85(1) of the 1983 Act.

38-29   Section 99 is now s. 113 of the 1983 Act.

38-30   Section 100 is now s. 114 of the 1983 Act.

38-31   Section 101 is now s. 115 of the 1983 Act. Section 138(3) is now s. 158(3) of that Act, and s. 139 is now s. 159 of that Act.

38-32   Footnote 43. Section 147 is now s. 169 of the 1983 Act; s. 149(1) is now s. 172(3) of that Act.

38-33   Section 140(4) is now s. 160(4) of the 1983 Act. Section 139(1) to (3) is now s. 159(1) to (3) of that Act.
Footnote 44. Section 152 is now s. 174 of the 1983 Act; s. 145 is now s. 167 of that Act.

38-34   Section 99(1) and (2) is now s. 93(1) and (2) of the 1983 Act. Notification of a parliamentary vacancy arising during a recess is now made in the *London Gazette* in accordance with the Recess Elections Act 1975.

38-35   Footnote 45. Section 61(6) is now s. 73(6) of the 1983 Act.
Footnote 46. Section 72 is now s. 84 of the 1983 Act.
Footnote 47. Section 66(3) is now s. 78(3) of the 1983 Act; s. 80 is now s. 92 of that Act; s. 95(3) is now s. 110(3) of that Act.

38-36   The relevant parts of s. 48 are now s. 61 of the 1983 Act. Section 168(2) is re-enacted with some ve₁oal alterations by s. 190 of the 1983 Act. "Voting papers" are now called "ballot papers". Maximum penalty on summary conviction now three months' imprisonment or a fine of level 2.

38-37   Section 153(2) is now s. 175(2) of the 1983 Act.
Footnote 49. Section 96 is now s. 111 of the 1983 Act.
Footnote 50. Section 153(1) is now s. 175(1) of the 1983 Act.

38-38   Section 91(1) is re-enacted by s. 106(1), (2), (5) and (6) of the 1983 Act with some verbal alterations. Section 106(1) and (2) does not apply to the election of councillors in Scotland: 1983 Act, s. 106(4). Section 81 is now s. 94 of the 1983 Act.

38-39   Section 92 is now s. 107 of the 1983 Act.

38-40   Section 84 is re-enacted by s. 97 of the Representation of the People Act 1983. Section 97(3) provides:

> "(3) If a constable reasonably suspects any person of committing an offence under subsection (1) above, he may if requested so to do by the chairman of the meeting require that person to declare to him immediately his name and address and, if that person refuses or fails so to declare his name and address or gives a false name and address, he shall be liable on summary conviction to a fine not exceeding level 1 on the standard scale, and—
> (a) if he refuses or fails so to declare his name and address or
> (b) if the constable reasonably suspects him of giving a false name and address,
> the constable may without warrant arrest him."

38-41   Section 52 is now s. 65 of the 1983 Act.

38-42   Section 49 is now s. 62 of the 1983 Act, and extends to a patient's declaration: see 1983 Act, s. 7, as well as to a service declaration. Breach of s. 62 is a summary offence; maximum penalty six months' imprisonment and a fine of level 4.

38-43   Section 50 is now s. 63 of the 1983 Act: maximum penalty a fine of level 3. Section 63(4) provides that nothing in s. 63 "imposes liability to summary prosecution on a returning officer for a Parliamentary election in Scotland or on a person under a duty to discharge the functions of such a returning officer".

Section 51 is now s. 64 of the 1983 Act. Section 64(2) provides that no person to whom the section applies shall be liable to any penalty at common law or to any action of damages in respect of breach of his official duty.

Section 53 is now s. 66 of the 1983 Act.

Section 86 is now s. 99 of the 1983 Act: maximum penalty a fine of level 4. The references to sheriff clerks, etc. were originally removed by the Returning Officers (Scotland) Act 1977.

Section 87 is now s. 100 of the 1983 Act.

38-44   Section 129 is now s. 149 of the 1983 Act. The affidavits are those referred to in s. 148 of that Act.

38-45   Section 155(1) is now s. 178(1) of the 1983 Act. The term "British subject" is replaced by "Commonwealth citizen": see British Nationality Act 1981, s. 37.

38-46   Section 156 is now s. 179 of the 1983 Act; s. 95 is now s. 110 of the 1983 Act.

Footnote 58. Sections 63(6), 91 and 80(3) are now respectively ss. 75(6), 106 and 92(3) of the 1983 Act.

CHAPTER 39

SEDITION AND ALLIED OFFENCES

39-09   The Unlawful Oaths Act 1797 and the Unlawful Oaths Act 1812 are repealed by the Statute Law (Repeals) Act 1981.

39-10   The Prevention of Terrorism (Temporary Provisions) Act 1976 is repealed and replaced by the Prevention of Terrorism (Temporary Provisions) Act 1984, which makes the following provisions regarding proscribed organisations:

"**1.**—(1) Subject to subsection (7) below, if any person—

(*a*)   belongs or professes to belong to a proscribed organisation;

(*b*)   solicits or invites financial or other support for a proscribed organisation, or knowingly makes or receives any contribution in money or otherwise to the resources of a proscribed organisation; or

(*c*)   arranges or assists in the arrangement or management of, or addresses, any meeting of three or more persons (whether or not it is a meeting to which the public are admitted) knowing that the meeting—

(i)   is to support a proscribed organisation;

(ii)   is to further the activities of such an organisation; or

(iii)   is to be addressed by a person belonging or professing to belong to such an organisation,

he shall be guilty of an offence.

(2) A person guilty of an offence under subsection (1) above shall be liable—

(*a*)   on summary conviction to imprisonment for a term not exceeding six months, or to a fine not exceeding the [prescribed sum], or both; or

(*b*)   on conviction on indictment to imprisonment for a term not exceeding five years, or to a fine, or both.

(3) Any organisation for the time being specified in Schedule 1 to this Act is a proscribed organisation for the purposes of this Act; and any organisation which passes under a name mentioned in that Schedule shall be treated as proscribed, whatever relationship (if any) it has to any other organisation of the same name.

(4) The Secretary of State may by order made by statutory instrument add to Schedule 1 to this Act any organisation that appears to him to be concerned in terrorism occurring in the United Kingdom and connected with Northern Irish affairs, or in promoting or encouraging it.

(5) The Secretary of State may also by order so made remove an organisation from Schedule 1 to this Act.

(6) In this section and section 2 below 'organisations' includes any association or combination of persons.

(7) A person belonging to a proscribed organisation shall not be guilty of an offence under this section by reason of belonging to the organisation if he shows—

(*a*)   that he became a member when it was not a proscribed organisation under the current legislation; and

(*b*)   that he has not since he became a member taken part in any of its activities at any time while it was a proscribed organisation under that legislation.

(8) In subsection (7) above 'the current legislation', in relation to any time, means whichever of the following was in force at that time—

    (*a*) the Prevention of Terrorism (Temporary Provisions) Act 1974;

    (*b*) the Prevention of Terrorism (Temporary Provisions) Act 1976;

    (*c*) this Act.

(9) The reference in subsection (7) above to a person becoming a member of an organisation is a reference to the only or last occasion on which he became a member.

(10) The court by or before which a person is convicted of an offence under this section may order the forfeiture of any money or other property which, at the time of the offence, he had in his possession or under his control for the use or benefit of the proscribed organisation.

    2.—(1) Any person who in a public place—

    (*a*) wears any item of dress; or

    (*b*) wears, carries or displays any article,

in such a way or in such circumstances as to arouse reasonable apprehension that he is a member or supporter of a proscribed organisation, shall be guilty of an offence, and shall be liable on summary conviction—

    (i) to imprisonment for a term not exceeding six months; or

    (ii) to a fine of an amount not exceeding level 5 on the standard scale,

or to both.

(2) A constable may arrest without warrant anyone whom he has reasonable grounds to suspect of being a person guilty of an offence under this section.

(3) In this section 'public place' includes any highway and any other premises or place to which at the material time the public have, or are permitted to have, access, whether on payment or otherwise."

The proscribed organisations are the Irish Republican Army and the Irish National Liberation Army: *ibid.*, Sched. 1.

Section 10 of the Act prohibits the collection of money for terrorist activities, and provides:

    "(1) If any person—

    (*a*) solicits or invites any other person to give, lend or otherwise make available, whether for consideration or not, any money or other property; or

    (*b*) receives or accepts from any other person, whether for consideration or not, any money or other property,

intending that it shall be applied or used for or in connection with the commission, preparation or instigation of acts of terrorism to which this Part of this Act applies, he shall be guilty of an offence.

(2) If any person gives, lends or otherwise makes available to any other person, whether for consideration or not, any money or other property, knowing or suspecting that it will or may be applied or used for or in connection with the commission, preparation or instigation of acts of terrorism to which this Part of this Act applies, he shall be guilty of an offence."

Maximum penalty 5 years' imprisonment and a fine on indictment, six months and a fine on summary conviction, and forfeiture of any property which the offender had at the time of the offence and intended to use for terrorist purposes: s. 10(3), (4).

Section 11, which requires disclosure of information regarding terrorism (*cf. H.M. Advocate* v. *Von*, 1979 S.L.T. (Notes) 62), provides:

39-10 "(1) If a person who has information which he knows or believes might be of material assistance—

    (*a*) in preventing the commission by any other person of an act of terrorism to which this Part of this Act applies, or

    (*b*) in securing the apprehension, prosecution or conviction of any other person for an offence involving the commission, preparation or instigation of an act of terrorism to which this Part of this Act applies,

fails without reasonable excuse to disclose that information as soon as reasonably practicable—

    (i) in England and Wales, to a constable;

    (ii) in Scotland, to a constable or the procurator fiscal, or

    (iii) in Northern Ireland, to a constable or a member of Her Majesty's forces,

he shall be guilty of an offence . . .

(3) Proceedings for an offence under this section may be taken, and the offence may for the purpose of those proceedings be treated as having been committed, in any place where the offender is or has at any time been since he first knew or believed that the information might be of material assistance as mentioned in subsection (1) above."

Maximum penalty as for s. 10, *supra*, except for forfeiture.

Both section 10 and s. 11 apply to acts of terrorism occurring in the United Kingdom and connected with Northern Irish affairs: s. 10(5).

Section 6 of the Act empowers the Secretary of State to exclude from the United Kingdom persons, other than British citizens, who have been concerned with terrorism anywhere or are or may be attempting to enter Great Britain or Northern Ireland in connection with acts of terrorism. Failure to comply with an exclusion order is an offence, and it is also an offence to harbour, or be knowingly concerned in the entry to the United Kingdom of, a person subject to such an order: s. 9; maximum penalty as for s. 11, *supra*.

For hijacking, see *supra*, para. 16-19.

For the offence of taking hostages, see *supra*, para. 29-54a.

For the offence of threatening protected persons, see *supra*, para. 29-65.

39-12   Section 84 of the Representation of the People Act 1949 is re-enacted by s. 97 of the Representation of the People Act 1983.

39-17   For an English definition of breach of the peace, see *R. v. Howell (Errol)* [1982] Q.B. 416.

See also *Simcock* v. *Rhodes* (1978) 66 Cr. App. R. 192; *Parkin* v. *Norman* [1983] Q.B. 92.

The garden of a house through which access is gained to the house is not a public place: *R. v. Edwards* (1978) 67 Cr. App. R. 228; see also *Marsh* v. *Arnott* (1982) 75 Cr. App. R. 211.

39-23   For the meaning of "persistently follows" and "following in a disorderly manner", see *Elsey* v. *Smith*, 1982 S.C.C.R. 218, where the following was done by a car on a motorway "in order to follow somebody else, and . . . in order to achieve that object, . . . persistently [driving] near to that other person, in company with two other vehicles similarly engaged, and on occasions [altering] one's speed so as to require that other person to overtake": at 229. One determined

39-23 effort to follow over a substantial distance may constitute persistent following: *ibid*. Following of a kind which is calculated to, and does, distress and harass, and which could have been restrained by interdict, is wrongful: *Elsey* v. *Smith* (*supra*).

"Wrongful" means contrary to the law, and an act which is protected from civil proceedings because it is carried out in an industrial dispute does not thereby cease to be wrongful for the purposes of a prosecution under s. 7: *Galt* v. *Philp*, 1984 S.L.T. 28.

Watching and besetting may be carried out from inside the premises in question: *ibid*.

39-26 Section 15 of the Trade Union and Labour Relations Act 1974, as substituted by s. 16 of the Employment Act 1980 and amended by Sched. 3 to the Employment Act 1982, is in the following terms:

"(1) It shall be lawful for a person in contemplation or furtherance of a trade dispute to attend—
> (*a*) at or near his own place of work, or
> (*b*) if he is an official of a trade union, at or near the place of work of a member of that union whom he is accompanying and whom he represents,

for the purpose only of peacefully obtaining or communicating information, or peacefully persuading any person to work or abstain from working.

(2) If a person works or normally works—
> (*a*) otherwise than at any one place, or
> (*b*) at a place the location of which is such that attendance there for a purpose mentioned in subsection (1) above is impracticable,

his place of work for the purposes of that subsection shall be any premises of his employer from which he works or from which his work is administered.

(3) In the case of a worker who is not in employment where—
> (*a*) his last employment was terminated in connection with a trade dispute, or
> (*b*) the termination of his employment was one of the circumstances giving rise to a trade dispute, subsection (1) above shall in relation to that dispute have effect as if any reference to his place of work were a reference to his former place of work.

(4) A person who is an official of a trade union by virtue only of having been elected or appointed to be a representative of some of the members of the union shall be regarded for the purposes of subsection (1) above as representing only those members; but otherwise an official of a trade union shall be regarded for those purposes as representing all its members."

39-28 Section 29 of the Trade Union and Labour Relations Act 1974, as amended by the Employment Act 1982, s. 18, is in the following terms:

"**29.**—(1) In this Act 'trade dispute' means a dispute between workers and their employer, which relates wholly or mainly to one or more of the following, that is to say—
> (*a*) terms and conditions of employment, or the physical conditions in which any workers are required to work;
> (*b*) engagement or non-engagement, or termination or suspension of employment or the duties of employment, of one or more workers;
> (*c*) allocation of work or the duties of employment as between

workers or groups of workers;
(*d*) matters of discipline;
(*e*) the membership or non-membership of a trade union on the part of a worker;
(*f*) facilities for officials of trade unions; and
(*g*) machinery for negotiation or consultation, and other procedures, relating to any of the foregoing matters, including the recognition by employers or employers' associations of the right of a trade union to represent workers in any such negotiation or consultation or in the carrying out of such procedures.

(2) A dispute between a Minister of the Crown and any workers shall, notwithstanding that he is not the employer of those workers, be treated for the purposes of this Act as a dispute between those workers and their employer if the dispute relates—
(*a*) to matters which have been referred for consideration by a joint body on which, by virtue of any provision made by or under any enactment, that Minister is represented; or
(*b*) to matters which cannot be settled without that Minister exercising a power conferred on him by or under an enactment.

(3) There is a trade dispute for the purposes of this Act even though it relates to matters occurring outside the United Kingdom, so long as the person or persons whose actions in the United Kingdom are said to be in contemplation or furtherance of a trade dispute relating to matters occurring outside the United Kingdom are likely to be affected in respect of one or more of the matters specified in subsection (1) of this section by the outcome of that dispute.

(5) An act, threat or demand done or made by one person or organisation against another which, if resisted, would have led to a trade dispute with that other, shall, notwithstanding that because that other submits to the act or threat or accedes to the demand no dispute arises, be treated for the purposes of this Act as being done or made in contemplation of a trade dispute with that other.

(6) In this section—
'employment' includes any relationship whereby one person personally does work or performs services for another;
'worker', in relation to a dispute with an employer, means—
(*a*) a worker employed by that employer; or
(*b*) a person who has ceased to be employed by that employer where—
(i) his employment was terminated in connection with the dispute; or
(ii) the termination of his employment was one of the circumstances giving rise to the dispute.

(6) In the Conspiracy, and Protection of Property Act 1875 'trade dispute' has the same meaning as in this Act.''

CHAPTER 40

MOBBING

40-03 See also *Hancock* v. *H.M.A.*, 1981 J.C. 74.

40-13 In *Hancock* v. *H.M.A.*, 1981 J.C. 74, Lord Justice-General Emslie said, at page 86:

40-13　"I agree. A mob is essentially a combination of persons, sharing a common criminal purpose, which proceeds to carry out that purpose by violence, or by intimidation by sheer force of numbers. A mob has, therefore, a will and a purpose of its own, and all members of the mob contribute by their presence to the achievement of the mob's purpose, and to the terror of its victims, even where only a few directly engage in the commission of the specific unlawful acts which it is the mob's common purpose to commit. Where there has assembled a mob which proceeds to behave as a mob a question may arise whether all those present when it acts to achieve its common purpose are truly members of the mob or mere spectators. Membership of a mob is not to be inferred from proof of mere presence at the scene of its activities. The inference of membership is, however, legitimate if there is evidence that an individual's presence is a 'countenancing' or contributory presence, i.e., if his presence is for the purpose of countenancing or contributing to the achievement of the mob's unlawful objectives."

CHAPTER 41

BREACH OF THE PEACE, OBSCENE PUBLICATIONS AND BLASPHEMY

41-01　It is not a breach of the peace or any other crime merely to form part of a disorderly crowd in circumstances not amounting to mobbing: *MacNeill* v. *Robertson and Ors.*, 1982 S.C.C.R. 468. It is necessary to aver that the accused himself behaved in a disorderly manner, either directly, or impliedly, by averring that each member of the crowd so behaved: *Tudhope* v. *Morrison*, 1983 S.C.C.R. 262 (Sh. Ct.); *cf. Tudhope* v. *O'Neill*, 1983 S.C.C.R. 443.

41-02　See also *Elsey* v. *Smith*, 1982 S.C.C.R. 218; *supra*, para. 39-23.

41-04　It has been held to be a breach of the peace to shout pro-I.R.A. slogans outside Celtic Football Park, on the ground that many spectators would have found them highly provocative and inflammatory: *Duffield and Anr.* v. *Skeen*, 1981 S.C.C.R. 66; *cf. Alexander* v. *Smith*, 1984 S.L.T. 176. It has also been held to be a breach of the peace to direct offensive remarks and gestures towards rival supporters inside a football ground: *Wilson* v. *Brown*, 1982 S.C.C.R. 49. It can even be a breach of the peace to cause embarrassment: *Sinclair* v. *Annan*, 1980 S.L.T. (Notes) 55, where the accused addressed indecent remarks to a woman. On the other hand, it has been held not to be a breach of the peace merely to sniff glue when in a state of apparent oblivion to one's surroundings: *Fisher* v. *Keane*, 1981 J.C. 50.

　　Subject to certain exceptions it is an offence under s. 54 of the Civic Government (Scotland) Act 1982 for any person who plays an instrument, sings or performs or operates a sound producing device, so as to give other persons reasonable cause for annoyance to fail to desist on being required to do so by a uniformed constable: maximum penalty a fine of level 2; see also para. 47-11 in the main work.

It has been recently held in a number of cases that the common law crime of shameless indecency is committed by selling or exposing for sale (and perhaps even having for sale where there is also a charge of exposing for sale) articles which are obscene and "likely to deprave and corrupt the morals of the lieges and to create in their minds inordinate and lustful desires": *Robertson* v. *Smith*, 1980 J.C. 1; see *supra*, para. 1-32.

It is necessary for the Crown to show that the accused was aware of the obscene character of the article, and that his conduct was directed towards some person or persons with an intention or in the knowledge that it should corrupt or be calculated to corrupt them: *Dean* v. *John Menzies (Holdings) Ltd.*, 1981 J.C. 23, Lord Cameron at 32; *Tudhope* v. *Barlow*, 1981 S.L.T. (Sh. Ct.) 94. Nevertheless, the fact that the exposure is restricted to persons not under 18 years old, far from being a defence, is evidence of the accused's awareness of the obscene character of the material: *Robertson* v. *Smith, supra*; *Tudhope* v. *Taylor*, 1980 S.L.T. (Notes) 54; *Centrewall Ltd.* v. *MacNeill*, 1983 S.L.T. 326; *Smith* v. *Downie*, 1982 S.L.T. (Sh. Ct.) 23.

Books held as a reserve stock in a back shop or kept in drawers are "exposed for sale" if they are kept in immediate readiness for sale: *Scott* v. *Smith*, 1981 J.C. 46.

An averment that an article is "indecent and obscene" is tantamount to an averment that it is liable to corrupt and deprave, that being the common law meaning of "indecent and obscene": *Ingram* v. *Macari*, 1981 S.C.C.R. 184. Its tendency to corrupt and deprave is a matter of fact for the court, and not a matter for expert evidence: *Ingram* v. *Macari*, 1982 S.C.C.R. 372.

It is not an offence at common law for a wholesaler to have obscene articles in his possession for circulation to retailers: *Sommerville* v. *Tudhope*, 1981 J.C. 58; the premises in which the articles were kept in that case were not premises to which the public were invited to resort, and there was therefore "no affront to public decency or morals nor any action which of itself is designed or calculated to corrupt the morals of the lieges": Lord Cameron at 63.

It may, however, be a crime to distribute obscene material to retailers with intent that it be sold to the public, the crime being describable as "trafficking in obscene publications", although there is no example of such a crime, only a reference by Lord Cooper in *Galletly* v. *Laird,* 1953 J.C. 16 to traffic in pornography as an evil which obscenity legislation is designed to prevent: see *Sommerville* v. *Tudhope, supra*. Such distribution might constitute a conspiracy to commit shameless indecency, or make the wholesaler art and part in the retailer's shameless indecency once the latter had exposed the articles for sale.

Section 45 of the Civic Government (Scotland) Act 1982 allows local authorities to apply Sched. 2 to the Act, which empowers them to license sex shops, *i.e.* premises used for dealing in, or displaying or demonstrating, what are called sex articles: Sched. 2, para. 2(1). Such articles specifically include reading matter and vision or sound recordings portraying sexual activity or genital organs or intended to stimulate or encourage sexual activity: *ibid.*, para. 2(4). Local authorities are thus empowered to license the sale of pornography, but such licences are of no avail in a prosecution for shameless indecency or

41-16 obscenity, since para. 1 of Sched. 2 provides that nothing in the Schedule shall afford a defence to any charge except one under the Schedule itself (*e.g.* for breach of the licensing conditions) or be taken into account in any way in the trial of any such charge.

41-17 The relevant provisions of the Burgh Police (Scotland) Act 1892 and the corresponding provisions in local Acts are replaced by s. 51 of the Civic Government (Scotland) Act 1982, which provides, inter alia:

> "(2) Subject to subsection (4) below, any person who publishes, sells or distributes or, with a view to its eventual sale or distribution, makes, prints, has or keeps any obscene material shall be guilty of an offence under this section.
> (4) A person shall not be convicted of an offence under this section if he proves that he had used all due diligence to avoid committing the offence."

Maximum penalty a fine and two years' imprisonment on indictment, 3 months and a fine on summary conviction: s. 51(3). For a discussion of the law, see Keith Ewing, "Obscene Publications. Effect of the Civic Government (Scotland) Bill", 1982 S.L.T. (News) 55. For indecent displays, see *infra*, para. 41-25.

"Material" includes any book, magazine, bill, paper, print, film, tape, disc, or other kind of recording (whether of sound or visual images or both), photograph (positive or negative), drawing, painting, representation, model or figure: s. 51(8).

"Publishing" includes playing, projecting or otherwise reproducing: s. 51(8).

Section 51 does not apply to anything in a television broadcast by the BBC or IBA or any programme transmitted to the subscribers to a licensed diffusion service, or included in a play within the meaning of the Theatres Act 1968: s. 51(6).

41-21 Section 2(4)(*b*) of the Theatres Act 1968 is repealed by the Indecent Displays (Control) Act 1981. Section 380 of the Burgh Police (Scotland) Act 1892 is replaced by s. 51 of the Civic Government (Scotland) Act 1982, but no provision is made for a corresponding alteration in s.2(4)(*c*) of the Theatres Act, which is simply repealed by Sched. 8 to the Civic Government (Scotland) Act.

41-22 Section 1 of the Cinematograph Act 1909, as substituted by para. 1 of Sched. 1 to the Cinematograph (Amendment) Act 1982, prohibits the use of premises for cinematograph exhibitions unless they are licensed for the purpose under the Act. "Cinematograph exhibition" means any exhibition of moving pictures produced otherwise than by the simultaneous reception and exhibition of television programmes broadcast by the BBC or ITV or by a system licensed under s. 89 of the Post Office Act 1969. Exceptions are made for non-commercial exhibitions. The use of unlicensed premises for an exhibition requiring a licence is made an offence by s. 7(1)(*a*) of the Cinematograph (Amendment) Act 1982: maximum penalty a fine of £20,000; Cinematograph (Amendment) Act 1982, s. 7(4)(*a*); 1975 Act, s. 289D(1A)(*f*); Increase of Criminal Penalties etc. (Scotland) Order 1984.

41-22   Presentation of an obscene film may constitute shameless indecency: *Watt* v. *Annan*, 1978 J.C. 84; *supra*, para. 1-32. Films are also covered by s. 51 of the Civic Government (Scotland) Act 1982: *supra*, para. 41-17, *infra*, para. 41-25, which replaces earlier public and local legislation on obscenity.

Add new paragraph **41-22a**:

41-22a   *Indecent Photographs of Children.* Section 52 of the Civic Government (Scotland) Act 1982 provides:

> "(1) Any person who—
> (a) takes, or permits to be taken, any indecent photograph of a child (meaning, in this section a person under the age of 16);
> (b) distributes or shows such an indecent photograph;
> (c) has in his possession such an indecent photograph with a view to its being distributed or shown by himself or others; or
> (d) publishes or causes to be published any advertisement likely to be understood as conveying that the advertiser distributes or shows such an indecent photograph, or intends to do so
>
> shall be guilty of an offence under this section.
>
> (2) In proceedings under this section a person is to be taken as having been a child at any material time if it appears from the evidence as a whole that he was then under the age of 16 . . .
>
> (4) For the purpose of this section, a person is to be regarded as distributing an indecent photograph if he parts with possession of it to, or exposes or offers it for acquisition by, another person."

Maximum penalty two years' imprisonment on indictment: s. 52(3).

41-23   See also *Ingram* v. *Macari*, 1982 S.C.C.R. 372.

41-25   Delete original paragraph and substitute the following:

Indecent displays. The Indecent Advertisements Act 1889 is repealed by the Indecent Displays (Control) Act 1981, s. 1 of which, as amended by Sched. 1 to the Cinematograph (Amendment) Act 1982, provides:

> "(1) If any indecent matter is publicly displayed the person making the display and any person causing or permitting the display to be made shall be guilty of an offence.
>
> (2) Any matter which is displayed in or so as to be visible from any public place shall, for the purposes of this section, be deemed to be publicly displayed.
>
> (3) In subsection (2) above, 'public place', in relation to the display of any matter, means any place to which the public have or are permitted to have access (whether on payment or otherwise) while that matter is displayed except—
> (a) a place to which the public are permitted to have access only on payment which is or includes payment for that display; or
> (b) a shop or any part of a shop to which the public can only gain access by passing beyond an adequate warning notice;
>
> but the exclusions contained in paragraphs (a) and (b) above shall only apply where persons under the age of 18 years are not permitted to enter while the display in question is continuing.
>
> (4) Nothing in this section applies in relation to any matter—

(*a*) included in a television broadcast by the British Broadcasting Corporation or the Independent Broadcasting Authority or a programme transmitted to the premises of subscribers to a diffusion service licensed by the Secretary of State; or

(*b*) included in the display of an art gallery or museum and visible only from within the gallery or museum; or

(*c*) displayed by or with the authority of, and visible only from within a building occupied by, the Crown or any local authority; or

(*d*) included in a performance of a play (within the meaning of the Theatres Act 1968); or

(*e*) included in a cinematograph exhibition as defined in the Cinematograph Act 1909—

    (i) given in a place which as regards that exhibition is required to be licensed under section 2 of the Cinematograph Act 1909 or by virtue only of section 7 of that Act, is not required to be so licensed; or

    (ii) which is an exempted exhibition for the purpose of section 5 of the Cinematograph Act 1952 given by an exempted organisation as defined by section 5(4) of that Act.

(5) In this section 'matter' includes anything capable of being displayed, except that it does not include an actual human body or any part thereof; and in determining for the purpose of this section whether any displayed matter is indecent—

(*a*) there shall be disregarded any part of that matter which is not exposed to view; and

(*b*) account may be taken of the effect of juxtaposing one thing with another.

(6) A warning notice shall not be adequate for the purposes of this section unless it complies with the following requirements—

(*a*) The warning notice must contain the following words, and no others—

'WARNING

Persons passing beyond this notice will find material on display which they may consider indecent. No admittance to persons under 18 years of age.'

(*b*) The word 'WARNING' must appear as a heading.

(*c*) No pictures or other matter shall appear on the notice.

(*d*) The notice must be so situated that no one could reasonably gain access to the shop or part of the shop in question without being aware of the notice and it must be easily legible by any person gaining such access."

Maximum penalty two years' imprisonment and a fine on indictment, on summary conviction the prescribed sum in the sheriff court and a fine of level 3 in the district court: s. 4(2).

Nothing in this Act (except to the extent provided for by it) affects the law relating to shameless indecency or obscenity at common law or under s. 51 of the Civic Government (Scotland) Act 1982: Indecent Displays (Control) Act 1981, s. 5(4).

It is also an offence under s. 51(1) of the Civic Government (Scotland) Act 1982 to display any obscene material in any public place or in any other place where it can be seen by the public: maximum penalty three months' imprisonment and a fine on summary conviction, two years and a fine on indictment: s. 51(3). It is a defence to show due diligence to avoid the offence: s. 51(4). It remains to be seen

41-25 whether publishing warnings or restricting entry to premises will constitute due diligence, or simply be seen as evidence of the accused's knowledge that the material is obscene: *cf.* P.W. Ferguson, "The Limits of Statutory Obscenity", 1983 S.L.T. (News) 249; *Centrewall Ltd.* v. *MacNeill*, 1983 S.L.T. 326. It should be noted that any place to which the public are permitted to have access, whether on payment or otherwise, is a public place for the purpose of s. 51(1), so that that subsection can be contravened in circumstances which would not contravene the Indecent Displays (Control) Act 1981: Civic Government (Scotland) Act 1982, s. 51(8); *cf.* s. 133, *supra*, para. 36-41.

The Indecent Displays (Control) Act 1981 does not affect s. 51 of the Civic Government (Scotland) Act 1982: Indecent Displays (Control) Act 1981, s. 5(4)(*b*), as substituted by Civic Government (Scotland) Act 1982, s. 51(7), but a person charged under s. 51(1) may be convicted of a breach of the Indecent Displays (Control) Act 1981: Civic Government (Scotland) Act 1982, s. 51(5).

Section 51(1) does not apply to any matter in a television broadcast by the BBC or IBA or any programme transmitted to the subscribers to a licensed diffusion service, or included in a performance of a play within the meaning of the Theatres Act 1968: Civic Government (Scotland) Act 1982, s. 51(6).

"Material" has the same meaning in relation to offences under s. 51(1) as it has in relation to offences under s. 51(2); *supra*, para. 41-17.

41-28 Section 4 of the Vagrancy Act 1824 is repealed by the Civic Government (Scotland) Act 1982.

41-29 For a modern English case of blasphemy, see *R.* v. *Lemon* [1979] A.C. 617.

CHAPTER 43

DANGEROUS DRUGS

43-05 A controlled drug is any "substance or product" specified in the Schedules to the Act.

The descriptions in the Schedules are generic terms and include derivative forms of the drug named, so that, *e.g.* "cocaine" includes both the direct extracts of the coca-leaf and whatever results from a chemical transformation thereof: *R.* v. *Greensmith* [1983] 1 W.L.R. 1124.

43-06 The relevant sections of the Customs and Excise Act are now 50(1), 68(2) and 170 of the Customs and Excise Management Act 1979: *cf. R.* v. *Whitehead* [1982] Q.B. 1272.

43-07 Regulation 8 of the Misuse of Drugs Regulations 1973 permits the manufacture or compounding of drugs by a medical, dental or veterinary practitioner or pharmacist acting in his capacity as such, and the supply of drugs by such persons and other specified persons such as

43-07 nursing sisters and laboratory analysts to persons lawfully entitled to possess them.

43-08 Regulation 10 of the Misuse of Drugs Regulations 1973 permits the persons specified in regulation 8 thereof (*supra*, para. 43-07) to possess drugs for the purpose of acting in their capacity as such persons. Whether a doctor who administers drugs to himself is doing so in his capacity as a practitioner is a question of fact: *R. v. Dunbar* [1981] 1 W.L.R. 1536.

"Supply" means "transfer physical control." Where, therefore, X gives A a drug to keep for him, A supplies the drug to X when he returns it to him, although it has remained in X's ownership throughout: *R. v. Delgado* [1984] 1 W.L.R. 89.

43-09 The law now is that the only quantitative limitation is that of identifiability. It is an offence to be in possession of an identifiable quantity of a drug, whether or not it is so minute as to be unusable: *Keane v. Gallacher*, 1980 J.C. 77. The same view is now taken in England: *R. v. Boyesen* [1982] A.C. 768.

Footnote 18. Add after the reference to *McAttee v. Hogg*: *McRae v. H.M.A.*, 1975 J.C. 34: see also *Mingay v. MacKinnon*, 1980 J.C. 33.

43-10 A plant is cultivated when it is grown, and the term "cultivate" does not require that any particular care or labour be bestowed on it: *Tudhope v. Robertson*, 1980 J.C. 62. The evidence of cultivation in that case was "the positioning of the plants to secure the light necessary to growth, the condition of the plants, the presence of the seeds, and the objective which the respondents had in mind in having the plants in their house at all.": L.J-G. at 65-66.

43-11 It has been held in England that in view of the definition of cannabis as any part of any plant of the genus cannabis: para. 43-05, in the main work, to grow a cannabis plant is to produce the drug cannabis: *Taylor v. Chief Constable of Kent* [1981] 1 W.L.R. 606.

Footnote 31. Add: *R. v. Josephs and Christie* (1977) 65 Cr. App. R. 253.

43-13 The existence of s. 28 of the Misuse of Drugs Act 1971 does not affect the onus on the Crown to prove that the accused had possession of the drug, in the sense in which possession is defined in *R. v. Warner* [1969] A.C. 256: see para. 3-38 in the main work; *McKenzie v. Skeen*, 1983 S.L.T. 121; *R. v. Ashton-Rickhardt* [1978] 1 W.L.R. 37. But once it is proved that cannabis has been cultivated it is for the accused to show that he did not know it was cannabis: *R. v. Champ* (1981) 73 Cr. App. R. 367.

43-14 The Misuse of Drugs (Designation) Order 1973 is repealed and replaced by the Misuse of Drugs (Designation) Order 1977.

OFFENCES IN CONNECTION WITH OFFICIALS

44-08   Where it is proved that any money, gift or other consideration has been paid or given to or received by a person in public employment by or from a person seeking a contract from the public body concerned, there is a presumption of corruption: Prevention of Corruption Act 1916, s. 2; see *e.g. R. v. Braithwaite* [1983] 1 W.L.R. 385.

It was said in *R. v. Mills* (1978) 68 Cr. App. R. 154 that to receive money only with the intention of entrapping the giver was not to receive it with any intention of keeping it, and such money was therefore not received in breach of s. 2 of the Prevention of Corruption Act 1916.

It is no defence that while the accused knew that what he was given was intended as a bribe he did not accept it as such but as a reward for work done in the past: *R. v. Mills, supra.*

44-09   See now Customs and Excise Management Act 1979, s. 15.

44-12   See now Representation of the People Act 1983.

CHAPTER 46

BETTING, GAMING AND LOTTERIES

46-04   Section 10 of the Betting and Gaming Duties Act 1972 is repealed by the Betting and Gaming Duties Act 1981, and re-enacted by s. 10 of that Act.

46-22   See *Poole Stadium Ltd.v. Squires* [1982] 1 W.L.R. 235.

46-32   An advertisement placed inside a betting office window but read-able only from outside is published outside: *Windsors Ltd. v. Oldfield* [1981] 1 W.L.R. 1176. An advertisement which draws attention to the facilities available in a betting office is in breach of the section even if it does not say that the premises to which it is affixed are a betting office: *ibid.*

46-69   It is not necessary for there to be a lottery that the prizes are provided out of money contributed by the participants; it is enough that chances in the lottery are secured by some payment by the participants, such as the purchase of a packet of cigarettes which contains a lottery ticket: *Imperial Tobacco Ltd v. Att.-Gen.* [1981] A.C. 718.

CHAPTER 47

POLLUTION

47-03   Sections 31 and 32 of the Control of Pollution Act 1974 are still not in force, and pollution of rivers is still dealt with under s. 22 of the Rivers (Prevention of Pollution) (Scotland) Act 1951: see *Lockhart* v. *N.C.B.*, 1981 S.L.T. 161.

Section 50 of the Water (Scotland) Act 1946 is now s. 33 of the Water (Scotland) Act 1980.

47-06   Both owner and master are liable to prosecution for breach of s. 2(1): *Davies* v. *Smith*, 1983 S.C.C.R. 232.

CHAPTER 48

PERJURY AND ALLIED OFFENCES

48-09   The earlier Oaths Acts are repealed and re-enacted in the Oaths Act 1978, s. 5 of which provides:

> "(1) Any person who objects to being sworn shall be permitted to make his solemn affirmation instead of taking an oath.
>
> (2) Subsection (1) above shall apply in relation to a person to whom it is not reasonably practicable without inconvenience or delay to administer an oath in the manner appropriate to his religious belief as it applies in relation to a person objecting to be sworn.
>
> (3) A person who may be permitted under subsection (2) above to make his solemn affirmation may also be required to do so.
>
> (4) A solemn affirmation shall be of the same force and effect as an oath."

48-15
48-17   See also *Aitchison* v. *Simon*, 1976 S.L.T. (Sh. Ct.) 73.

48-18   It was held by the Judicial Committee in *Tsang Ping-Nam* v. *The Queen* [1981] 1 W.L.R. 1462 that it is not an attempt to pervert the course of justice for a witness giving "Queen's Evidence" to resile from his original witness statement which had not been on oath.

48-34   It has been held in England that to give a person one knows to be a suspected criminal the registration numbers of unmarked police cars in order to assist his escape is an attempt to pervert the course of justice even where the giver does not know of the suspect's guilt, and does not act corruptly, dishonestly or threateningly: *R.* v. *Thomas (Derek)* [1979] Q.B. 326.

48-36   It has been held in England to be an attempt to pervert the course of justice for an accused to interfere with his portion of a blood specimen before sending it for analysis, with intent to pervert the course of

48-36 justice, but without doing anything further. This was on the view that the resultant false analysis would be bound to be communicated to the accused's solicitor or the police, so that there was risk of injustice, and that that risk was sufficient to constitute the offence: *R. v. Murray (Gordon)* [1982] 1 W.L.R. 475.

48-38 It is an offence to induce one's solicitor to provide a court with false information in a plea in mitigation: *H.M.A. v. Murphy*, 1978 J.C. 1.

48-40 Once investigations have begun with a view to identifying the culprit in an offence which is known to have been committed, the giving of any false information to the police may constitute an attempt to pervert the course of justice, as in *Dean* v. *Stewart*, 1980 S.L.T. (Notes) 85 where the driver of a car (which had failed to stop after an accident) and another man pretended that the other man had been driving the car. It seems, therefore, that to tell lies to the police when interviewed by them in the course of criminal investigation is a crime.

It has been held in England that it is not an attempt to pervert the course of justice to have endorsements removed from the DVLC records where this is not done with intent to interfere with any pending or imminent proceedings or investigations which might lead to proceedings: *R. v. Selvage* [1982] Q.B. 372.

CHAPTER 49

ESCAPES FROM LAWFUL CUSTODY

49-09 See *e.g. Allan James Cairns Peden*, Criminal Appeal Court, March 1978, unreported, where someone who was under arrest tried to run away from the arresting officer; he was convicted of attempting to pervert the course of justice.

49-16 In *Miln* v. *Stirton*, 1982 S.L.T. (Sh. Ct.) 11, unreported, it was held that a charge against a wife of attempting to defeat the ends of justice by harbouring her husband against whom, as she knew, there was an outstanding extract conviction warrant for his arrest, was incompetent; the sheriff followed Hume, i.49 and Alison, i.669. See now, however, *Smith* v. *Watson*, 1982 S.C.C.R. 15, *supra*, para. 20-05.

49-17 A person who knowingly compels, persuades, incites or assists a child who has been committed to care under s. 23(1) or 29(3) of the Children and Young Persons Act 1969 to become or continue to be absent from the premises where he is required to be by the relevant local authority is guilty of a summary offence: Child Care Act 1980, s. 16(1); maximum penalty six months' imprisonment and a fine of level 5.

CHAPTER 50

OFFENCES IN CONNECTION WITH JUDICIAL OFFICIALS

50-04   See also *Maxwell* v. *H.M.A.*, 1980 J.C. 40.

CHAPTER 51

CONTEMPT OF COURT

51-01   Footnote 2. *H.M.A.* v. *Airs* is now reported at 1975 J.C. 64.

51-04   For a witness to be guilty of prevarication he must be shown to be deliberately refusing to give evidence it is proved he was able to give: *Childs* v. *McLeod*, 1981 S.L.T. (Notes) 27. For the procedure in dealing with such a witness, see *Hutchison* v. *H.M.A.*, 1983 S.C.C.R. 504.

   Add new paragraph **51-04a**:

51-04a   Section 10 of the Contempt of Court Act 1981, which affects the decision in *H.M.A.* v. *Airs*, 1975 J.C. 64, provides:

> "No court may require a person to disclose, nor is any person guilty of contempt of court for refusing to disclose, the source of information contained in a publication for which he is responsible, unless it be established to the satisfaction of the court that disclosure is necessary in the interests of justice or national security or for the prevention of disorder or crime."

51-06   The maximum penalty under s. 344 is now a fine of level 3 or twenty-one days' imprisonment: Criminal Justice Act 1982, Sched. 7. Presumably conduct covered by the section should be prosecuted under the section, and not under the general law of contempt which provides for greater penalties: see Contempt of Court Act 1981, s. 15(2).

51-10   It has been held in England that where documents are made available by a party under an order to produce them in proceedings it is a contempt of court for them to be made publicly available by the other party: *Home Office* v. *Harman* [1983] 1 A.C. 280.

51-11   To introduce references to an immediately pending trial for assaulting a patient with severe brain damage by trying to block her air supply into a television programme dealing with the issue of maintaining life-support systems for such patients may be a contempt of court, and will certainly be so if the references are such as to suggest that the accused was carrying out a policy of withdrawing such support: *Atkins* v. *London Weekend Television Ltd.*, 1978 J.C. 48, a rare case where the prosecution was abandoned because of the contempt. Where

51-11 prosecutions have continued after contempt by prejudicial publicity they have been held to be competent on the ground that the contempt occurred some time before the trial so that its continuing effect, if any, could be countered by appropriate directions to the jury: *Stuurman* v. *H.M.A.*, 1980 J.C. 111; *H.* v. *Sweeney*, 1983 S.L.T. 48. For cases in summary procedure, see *Tudhope* v. *Glass*, 1981 S.C.C.R. 336; *Aitchison* v. *Bernardi*, 1984 S.C.C.R. 88.

The court in *Atkins, supra*, recognised it as part of the common law that prejudice which is an incidental and unintended by-product of a discussion of public affairs is not contempt, and s. 5 of the Contempt of Court Act 1981 now provides that a publication made as part of a discussion in good faith of public affairs or other matters of general public interest is not to be treated as contempt under the strict liability rule if the risk of impediment or prejudice to particular legal proceedings is merely incidental to the discussion. This defence would not have succeeded in *Atkins*, since the reference to the particular case was specific and deliberate. The court might also have held that in any event in the circumstances responsibility did not depend on the strict liability rule but on recklessness, since they described the respondents as having "undoubtedly chose[n] to sail very close to the wind and [taken] what they must have recognised was a calculated risk": at 56. Section 5 is at least in part a consequence of the decision of the European Court of Human Rights in *Sunday Times Ltd* v. *United Kingdom* [1979] 2 E.H.R.R. 245 in which the decision of the House of Lords in *Att.-Gen.* v. *Times Newspapers Ltd.* [1974] A.C. 273 was criticised. On the interpretation of s. 5 see *Att.-Gen.* v. *English* [1983] 1 A.C. 116.

Merely to report that a witness has been given police protection and is being kept during a trial at a secret address where this is in fact so, is not a contempt: *Kemp, Petr.*; *The Scotsman Publications Ltd., Petrs.*, 1982 S.C.C.R. 1.

Footnote 37. Add: *Atkins* v. *London Weekend Television Ltd.*, 1978 J.C. 48; *H.M.A.* v. *George Outram & Co. Ltd.*, 1980 J.C. 51.

51-12 It was held in the Full Bench case of *Hall* v. *Associated Newspapers Ltd.*, 1979 J.C. 1 (see Angela M. MacLean, "Contempt in Criminal Process", 1978 S.L.T. (News) 257) that the court's jurisdiction in contempt begins when the accused is arrested or when a warrant for his arrest is granted, or (in summary proceedings) from the service of the complaint, whichever is earliest. The statement in *Stirling* v. *Associated Newspapers Ltd.* that jurisdiction arises the moment a crime is committed was rejected by the court in *Hall*. They held, however, that it was not a defence that the offenders were unaware that there had been an arrest or that an arrest warrant had been issued, but that statement must now be read subject to the Contempt of Court Act 1981; see *infra*, para. 51-14a.

Where the statement complained of is made with the intention of creating prejudice it may, of course, be punishable as a contempt or as an attempt to pervert the course of justice, at whatever stage of the investigation it is made, or even if it is made before any investigation has begun: *supra*, para. 48-40; *Hall, supra*, L.J.-G. at 15; *Skeen* v. *Farmer*, 1980 S.L.T. (Sh. Ct.) 133; Contempt of Court Act 1981, s. 6(*c*).

51-14   The need for the contempt to be deliberate was stressed in a number of recent cases involving the failure of solicitors to appear timeously in court: *Macara* v. *MacFarlane*, 1980 S.L.T. (Notes) 26; *McKinnon* v. *Douglas*, 1982 S.C.C.R. 80. Where the solicitor arranges his affairs so as deliberately to take the risk of delaying proceedings by being late, he may be guilty of contempt: *Muirhead* v. *Douglas*, 1979 S.L.T. (Notes) 17.

Add new paragraphs **51-14a** to **15-14e**:

51-14a   CONTEMPT OF COURT ACT 1981. Sections 1 to 6 of this Act limit the application of the rule that *mens rea* is unnecessary in relation to conduct which constitutes contempt as tending to interfere with the course of justice in particular legal proceedings, which the Act calls "the strict liability rule."

Section 2 provides:

> "(1) The strict liability rule applies only in relation to publications, and for this purpose 'publication' includes any speech, writing, broadcast or other communication in whatever form, which is addressed to the public at large or any section of the public.
>
> (2) The strict liability rule applies only to a publication which creates a substantial risk that the course of justice in the proceedings in question will be seriously impeded or prejudiced.
>
> (3) The strict liability rule applies to a publication only if the proceedings in question are active within the meaning of this section at the time of the publication.
>
> (4) Schedule 1 applies for determining the times at which proceedings are to be treated as active within the meaning of this section."

"Proceedings" include proceedings in any tribunal or body exercising the judicial power of the State; proceedings before United Kingdom courts sitting in Scotland, as well as before the House of Lords in appeals from any court sitting in Scotland are treated as Scottish proceedings: s. 19.

Criminal proceedings (*i.e.* proceedings against a person in respect of an offence, other than appellate proceedings) are active from the stage of arrest or the grant of a warrant for arrest, or from the grant of a warrant to cite, or from the service of an indictment or other document specifying a charge, whichever is the earliest, until they are concluded by acquittal or sentence, or by any other order putting an end to the proceedings, or by discontinuance or operation of law: Sched. 1, paras. 3 to 5. "Sentence" includes a deferred sentence under ss. 219 or 432 of the 1975 Act, so that the strict liability rule may cease to apply before the accused is actually disposed of: Sched. 1, para. 6. The Act specifically provides that express abandonment or desertion simpliciter constitutes a discontinuance: *ibid.*, para. 7(*b*), so it appears that desertion *pro loco et tempore* does not. A finding of insanity in bar of trial constitutes a discontinuance of the proceedings, but they become active again if they are resumed: *ibid.*, para. 10(*a*).

Where proceedings begin with the grant of an arrest warrant, they cease to be active after twelve months if there has been no arrest, but revive with a subsequent arrest: *ibid.*, para. 11.

Appellate proceedings are active from the time they are begun by

51-14a notice of appeal or application for a stated case until they are "dispossed of or abandoned, discontinued or withdrawn": *ibid.*, para. 15. When the appeal court remits the case to the lower court or grants authority for a retrial, any further or new proceedings become active from the conclusion of the appeal proceedings: *ibid.*, para. 16.

51-14b Section 3 of the Contempt of Court Act 1981 provides a specific defence of reasonable care which limits the application of the strict liability rule even in those cases where it applies by reason of s. 2 of the Act. It provides:

> "(1) A person is not guilty of contempt of court under the strict liability rule as the publisher of any matter to which that rule applies if at the time of publication (having taken all reasonable care) he does not know and has no reason to suspect that relevant proceedings are active.
>
> (2) A person is not guilty of contempt of court under the strict liability rule as the distributor of a publication containing any such matter if at the time of distribution (having taken all reasonable care) he does not know that it contains such matter and has no reason to suspect that it is likely to do so.
>
> (3) The burden of proof of any fact tending to establish a defence afforded by this section to any person lies upon that person."

51-14c The strict liability rule does not apply to publication as part of a bona fide discussion of matters of public interest if the risk of prejudice is merely incidental: Contempt of Court Act 1981, s. 5; see *supra*, para. 51-11.

51-14d Section 6 of the Contempt of Court Act 1981 specifically provides that the preceding sections of the Act will not (*a*) prejudice any common law defence to strict liability contempt, (*b*) make any publication a contempt which would not otherwise have been so, or (*c*) restrict liability for contempt in respect of conduct intended to impede or prejudice the administration of justice.

51-14e The maximum penalty for contempt is now two years' imprisonment and a fine where the contempt relates to proceedings on indictment. In relation to summary proceedings it is three months' imprisonment and a fine of level 4 in the sheriff court and sixty days and a fine of level 4 in the district court: Contempt of Court Act 1981, s. 15(2); Criminal Justice Act 1982, Sched. 7. It is no longer competent to order a person to be detained until he purges his contempt, but the court may discharge the offender before the conclusion of the fixed term of imprisonment imposed: *ibid.*, s. 15(1).

51-15 Section 9 of the Contempt of Court Act 1981 prohibits the use of sound recording devices in court without leave, except for the purpose of official transcripts. There is apparently no prohibition on making silent films. Section 9 provides:

> "(1) Subject to subsection (4) below, it is a contempt of court—
> (*a*) to use in court, or bring into court for use, any tape recorder or other instrument for recording sound, except with the leave of the court;

(b) to publish a recording of legal proceedings made by means of any such instrument, or any recording derived directly or indirectly from it, by playing it in the hearing of the public or any section of the public, or to dispose of it or any recording so derived, with a view to such publication;

(c) to use any such recording in contravention of any conditions of leave granted under paragraph (a).

(2) Leave under paragraph (a) of subsection (1) may be granted or refused at the discretion of the court, and if granted may be granted subject to such conditions as the court thinks proper with respect to the use of any recording made pursuant to the leave; and where leave has been granted the court may at the like discretion withdraw or amend it either generally or in relation to any particular of the proceedings.

(3) Without prejudice to any other power to deal with an act of contempt under paragraph (a) of subsection (1), the court may order the instrument, or any recording made with it, or both, to be forfeited; and any object so forfeited shall (unless the court otherwise determines on application by a person appearing to be the owner) be sold or otherwise disposed of in such manner as the court may direct.

(4) This section does not apply to the making or use of sound recordings for purposes of official transcripts of proceedings."

Add new paragraphs **51-15a** to **51-15c**:

51-15a CONTEMPT OF COURT ACT 1981. The common law rule is preserved by section 4(1) of the Contempt of Court Act 1981, which provides:

"(1) Subject to this section a person is not guilty of contempt of court under the strict liability rule in respect of a fair and accurate report of legal proceedings held in public, published contemporaneously and in good faith."

Publication may, however, be restricted by the court in terms of section 4(2) which provides:

"(2) In any such proceedings the court may, where it appears to be necessary for avoiding a substantial risk of prejudice to the administration of justice in those proceedings, or in any other proceedings pending or imminent, order that the publication of any report of the proceedings, or any part of the proceedings, be postponed for such period as the court thinks necessary for that purpose."

(See *R.* v. *Horsham JJ, ex p. Farquharson* [1982] Q.B. 762).
Publication of a report which is postponed by an order under s. 4(2) is contemporaneous if it is published as soon as practicable after the expiry of the order: s. 4(3)(a).

51-15b Where a court allows a name or other matter to be withheld from the public in court proceedings it may give such directions prohibiting its publication in connection with the proceedings as appear necessary for the purpose for which it was withheld: Contempt of Court Act 1981, s. 11.

51-15c   Section 8 of the Act renders jury deliberations confidential. It provides:

> "(1) Subject to subsection (2) below, it is a contempt of court to obtain, disclose or solicit any particulars of statements made, opinions expressed, arguments advanced or votes cast by members of a jury in the course of their deliberations in any legal proceedings.
> (2) This section does not apply to any disclosure of any particulars—
>> (*a*) in the proceedings in question for the purpose of enabling the jury to arrive at their verdict, or in connection with the delivery of that verdict, or
>> (*b*) in evidence in any subsequent proceedings for an offence alleged to have been committed in relation to the jury in the first mentioned proceedings,
>
> or to the publication of any particulars so disclosed."

51-17   Section 169 is rewritten by s. 22 of the Criminal Justice (Scotland) Act 1980, and now reads as follows:

> "(1) No newspaper report of any proceedings in a court shall reveal the name, address or school, or include any particulars calculated to lead to the identification, of any person under the age of 16 years concerned in the proceedings, either—
>> (*a*) as being a person against or in respect of whom the proceedings are taken; or
>> (*b*) as being a witness therein;
>
> nor shall any picture which is, or includes, a picture of a person under the age of 16 years so concerned in the proceedings be published in any newspaper in a context relevant to the proceedings:
> Provided that, in any case—
>> (i) where the person is concerned in the proceedings as a witness only and no one against whom the proceedings are taken is under the age of 16 years, the foregoing provisions of this subsection shall not apply unless the court so directs;
>> (ii) the court may at any stage of the proceedings if satisfied that it is in the public interest so to do, direct that the requirements of this section (including such requirements as applied by a direction under paragraph (i) above) shall be dispensed with to such extent as the court may specify;
>> (iii) the Secretary of State may, after completion of the proceedings, if so satisfied by order dispense with the said requirements to such extent as may be specified in the order.
>
> (2) This section shall, with the necessary modifications, apply in relation to sound and television broadcasts as it applies in relation to newspapers.
> (3) A person who publishes matter in contravention of this section shall be guilty of an offence and liable on summary conviction to a fine not exceeding [level 4 on the standard scale].
> (4) In this section, references to a court shall not include a court in England, Wales or Northern Ireland."

Section 365 of the 1975 Act is repealed by Sched. 8 to the Criminal Justice (Scotland) Act 1980.

51-18   Section 374 is rewritten by s. 22 of the Criminal Justice (Scotland) Act 1980, and is now in the same terms as s. 169 of the 1975 Act; *supra*, para. 51-17.

51-19   Add new paragraphs **51-20** and **51-21**:

51-20   *Fatal Accident Inquiries.* Section 4(4) of the Fatal Accidents and Sudden Deaths Inquiry (Scotland) Act 1976 empowers the sheriff to make an order prohibiting the publication of details leading to the identification of persons under the age of seventeen. Breach of such a prohibition is a summary offence: maximum penalty a fine of level 4: s. 4(5).

51-21   *Committal Proceedings.* It is an offence to publish anywhere in Britain any details of committal proceedings in England and Wales which result in the committal of anyone for trial until after the trial unless the magistrates' court on application by an accused permits publication: Magistrates' Courts Act 1980, s. 8; maximum penalty a fine of level 3. This prohibition does not extend to the limited information as to the names of those concerned, the place of committal and the charges involved set out in s. 8(4) of the Magistrates' Courts Act.

CHAPTER 52

GAME LAWS

52-04   Section 43(1) of the Agriculture (Scotland) Act 1948 is repealed by the Deer (Amendment) (Scotland) Act 1982, and is replaced by s. 33(3) to (4E) of the Deer (Scotland) Act 1959 as substituted by s. 13 of the said Act of 1982.

52-18   The provision quoted is now s. 22(1), and it applies also to intentionally injuring deer: Deer (Amendment) (Scotland) Act 1982, s. 6.

Section 22(2) makes it an offence, subject to s. 33, for any person without legal right to take or kill deer on any land, or without permission from someone having such right, to remove any deer carcase from that land: Deer (Amendment) (Scotland) Act 1982, s. 6(*c*). This provision follows on the decision in *Miln* v. *Maher*, 1979 J.C. 58 that "takes" in s. 22(1) refers to the capture of a live deer and does not extend to the removal of a deer one has killed: the maximum penalty for contravening any provision of s. 22 is now a fine of level 4 per deer or carcase and three months' imprisonment and forfeiture of the deer or carcase: Deer (Amendment) (Scotland) Act 1982, s. 6(3)(*c*); Sched. 1. The court may also cancel any firearm or shotgun certificate held by the offender: Deer (Scotland) Act 1959, s. 28A, as inserted by Deer (Amendment) (Scotland) Act, 1982, Sched. 2.

Maximum penalty under s. 24 is now a fine of level 5 per deer and six months' imprisonment, and forfeiture of the deer: Deer (Amendment) (Scotland) Act 1982, Sched. 1. Maximum penalty for preparatory acts is now a fine of level 4 and three months' imprisonment: Deer (Amendment) (Scotland) Act 1982, Sched. 1.

52-25   Footnote 79. The Protection of Birds Act 1954 is now replaced by the Wildlife and Countryside Act 1981, of which see Sched. 1.

52-26   Section 21 now applies to wilful injuring as well as to taking or killing: Deer (Amendment) (Scotland) Act 1982, s. 6(*a*).

Section 21 does not apply to the killing of deer by or on behalf of any person who keeps those deer by way of business on land enclosed by a deer-proof barrier for the production of meat or skins or other by-products, or as breeding stock, provided the deer are clearly marked to show that they are so kept: s. 21(5A) as inserted by Deer (Amendment) (Scotland) Act 1982, s. 7.

Maximum penalty is as for contraventions of s. 22: *supra*, para. 52-18.

52-29   For maximum penalty for preparatory acts, see *supra*, para. 52-18.

52-32   Section 23(2A) to (2C) of the Deer (Scotland) Act 1959, as inserted by s. 8(1) of the Deer (Amendment) (Scotland) Act 1982 provides:

> "Subject to subsection (2B) below and section 33(1) of this Act, if any person—
>> (*a*) discharges any firearm, or discharges or projects any missile, from any aircraft at any deer; or
>> (*b*) notwithstanding the provisions of section 23(5) of this Act uses any aircraft for the purpose of transporting any live deer other than in the interior of the aircraft,
> he shall be guilty of an offence.
>
> (2B) Nothing in subsection (2A)(*b*) above shall make unlawful anything done by, or under the supervision of, a veterinary surgeon or practitioner.
>
> (2C) In subsection (2B) above 'veterinary practitioner' means a person who is for the time being registered in the supplementary register, and 'veterinary surgeon' means a person who is for the time being registered in the register of veterinary surgeons."

For s. 33(1) see para. 52-18 in the main work.

Section 23A of the Deer (Scotland) Act 1959, as inserted by s. 10 of the Deer (Amendment) (Scotland) Act 1982, empowers the Secretary of State to make orders regarding the classes of firearms, ammunition, sights and other equipment which may lawfully be used to kill deer and the circumstances in which they may be so used. Breach of such an order is punishable by a fine of level 4 for each deer taken or killed and three months' imprisonment: s. 23A(3). The court may also cancel any firearm or shotgun certificate held by the offender: Deer (Scotland) Act 1959, s. 28A, as inserted by Deer (Amendment) (Scotland) Act 1982, Sched. 2.

Section 23A(5) makes it a summary offence to use any firearm or ammunition for the purpose of wilfully injuring deer: maximum penalty as above.

Add new paragraph **52-32a**:

52-32a   *Use of Vehicle to Drive Deer.* Section 23(3A) of the Deer (Scotland) Act 1959, as inserted by s. 9 of the Deer (Amendment) (Scotland) Act 1982, makes it an offence to use a vehicle to drive deer on unenclosed land with intent to take, kill or injure them: maximum penalty a fine of level 4 per deer and three months' imprisonment.

52-33   The Protection of Wild Birds Act 1954 is replaced by the Wildlife and Countryside Act 1981, and s. 5(1)(*d*) of the 1954 Act is now s. 5(1)(*c*) of that Act: *infra*, para. 52-36.

52-36   The Protection of Wild Birds Act 1954 is repealed by the Wildlife and Countryside Act 1981 and s. 5(1) of the 1954 Act is substantially re-enacted by s. 5 of that Act which provides:

"(1) Subject to the provisions of this Part, if any person—
   (*a*) sets in position any of the following articles, being an article which is of such a nature and is so placed as to be calculated to cause bodily injury to any wild bird coming into contact therewith, that is to say, any springe, trap, gin, snare, hook and line, any electrical device for killing, stunning or frightening or any poisonous, poisoned or stupefying substance;
   (*b*) uses for the purpose of killing or taking any wild bird any such article as aforesaid, whether or not of such a nature and so placed as aforesaid, or any net, baited board, bird-lime or substance of a like nature to bird-lime;
   (*c*) uses for the purpose of killing or taking any wild bird—
      (i) any bow or crossbow;
      (ii) any explosive other than ammunition for a firearm;
      (iii) any automatic or semi-automatic weapon;
      (iv) any shot-gun of which the barrel has an internal diameter at the muzzle of more than one and three-quarter inches;
      (v) any device for illuminating a target or any sighting device for night shooting;
      (vi) any form of artificial lighting or any mirror or other dazzling device;
      (vii) any gas or smoke not falling within paragraphs (*a*) and (*b*); or
      (viii) any chemical wetting agent;
   (*d*) uses as a decoy, for the purpose of killing or taking any wild bird, any sound recording or any live bird or other animal whatever which is tethered, or which is secured by means of braces or other similar appliances, or which is blind, maimed or injured; or
   (*e*) uses any mechanically propelled vehicle in immediate pursuit of a wild bird for the purpose of killing or taking that bird,
he shall be guilty of an offence and be liable to a special penalty."

The remainder of s. 5 of the Wildlife and Countryside Act 1981 is as follows:

"(2) Subject to subsection (3), the Secretary of State may by order, either generally or in relation to any kind of wild bird specified in the order, amend subsection (1) by adding any method of killing or taking wild birds or by omitting any such method which is mentioned in that subsection.

(3) The power conferred by subsection (2) shall not be exerciseable, except for the purpose of complying with an international obligation, in relation to any method of killing or taking wild birds which involves the use of a firearm.

(4) In any proceedings under subsection (1)(*a*) it shall be a defence to show that the article was set in position for the purpose of killing or taking, in the interests of public health, agriculture, forestry, fisheries or nature conservation, any wild animals which could be lawfully killed or taken by those means and that he took all reasonable precautions to prevent injury thereby to wild birds.

52-36   (5) Nothing in subsection (1) shall make unlawful—

    (*a*) the use of a cage-trap or net by an authorised person for the purpose of taking a bird included in Part II of Schedule 2;

    (*b*) the use of nets for the purpose of taking wild duck in a duck decoy which is shown to have been in use immediately before the passing of the Protection of Birds Act 1954; or

    (*c*) the use of a cage-trap or net for the purpose of taking any game bird if it is shown that the taking of the bird is solely for the purpose of breeding;

but nothing in this subsection shall make lawful the use of any net for taking birds in flight or the use for taking birds on the ground of any net which is projected or propelled otherwise than by hand."

52-36
52-37   Footnotes 9, 10. Maximum penalty now a fine of level 4: Criminal Justice Act 1982, Sched. 6.

52-39   Section 5(1)(*a*) of the Protection of Wild Birds Act 1954 is now s. 5(1)(*a*) of the Wildlife and Countryside Act 1981: *supra*, para. 52-36.

52-40   Section 5(1)(*a*) is now s. 5(1)(*a*) of the Wildlife and Countryside Act 1981, and s. 5(3) of the 1954 Act is now s. 5(1)(*e*) of that Act: see *supra*, para. 52-36.

CHAPTER 53

FISHING LAWS

53-08   The Salmon Fisheries (Scotland) Act 1828 is repealed by the Statute Law (Repeals) Act 1977.

The taking of trout by set lines was prohibited by the Trout (Scotland) Act 1860, and is therefore illegal under ss. 2(2) and 24(2) of the Salmon and Freshwater Fisheries (Scotland) Act 1951 which repealed the 1860 Act. Rods which are left lying on the ground with lines trailing in the water are set lines even though they are not secured to the ground in any way: *Lockhart* v. *Cowan and Anr.*, 1980 S.L.T. (Sh. Ct.) 91.

53-16   Footnote 41. Add: *Cf. Fishmongers' Company* v. *Bruce*, 1980 S.L.T. (Notes) 35.

53-27   Footnote 73. The Fisheries (Scotland) Act 1756 is repealed by the Statute Law (Repeals) Act 1978.

Footnote 74. The Sea Fish Industry Act 1970 is substantially repealed and replaced by the Fisheries Act 1981.

53-28   The prohibition imposed by s. 2(2)(*b*) of the Fishery Limits Act 1976 on fishing by foreign boats applies only to boats which have entered British waters for a recognised purpose; boats which have entered in order to fish illegally should be charged with illegal entry under section 2(2)(*a*): *Mackenzie* v. *Uribe*, 1983 S.C.C.R. 152.

53-30   Footnote 77. Maximum penalty now three months' imprisonment and a fine of level 5, and forfeiture: Criminal Justice Act 1982, Sched. 6.

53-31   Section 6 of the Sea Fish (Conservation) Act 1967 is amended by s. 23 of the Fisheries Act 1981, and s. 6(1A) gives power to prohibit the trans-shipment within British fishery limits of sea fish or any particular description of sea fish, being fish caught in any waters specified by order.

Section 1 of the Sea Fish (Conservation) Act 1967 is now as substituted by s. 19 of the Fisheries Act 1981.

53-33   Footnote 91. Maximum penalty six months' imprisonment and a fine of level 5: Criminal Justice Act 1982, Sched. 6.

53-37   The Whale Fisheries (Scotland) Act 1907 is repealed by the Fisheries Act 1981.

Footnotes 5 to 7, 8. Maximum penalty now £50,000 on summary conviction, a fine on indictment: Fisheries Act 1981, s. 35(3), (4).